I Carried a Watermelon

I Carried a Watermelon

DIRTY DANCING AND ME

KATY BRAND

ONE PLACE. MANY STORIES

HQ
An imprint of HarperCollinsPublishers Ltd
1 London Bridge Street
London SE1 9GF

www.harpercollins.co.uk

HarperCollinsPublishers
1st Floor, Watermarque Building, Ringsend Road
Dublin 4, Ireland

This edition 2021

1
First published in Great Britain by
HQ, an imprint of HarperCollins*Publishers* Ltd 2019

Copyright © Katy Brand 2019

Katy Brand asserts the moral right to be
identified as the author of this work.
A catalogue record for this book is
available from the British Library.

ISBN: 9780008352820

MIX
Paper from
responsible sources
FSC™ C007454

This book is produced from independently certified FSC™ paper
to ensure responsible forest management.

For more information visit: www.harpercollins.co.uk/green

This book is set in 12/17 pt. Sabon

Printed and bound in Great Britain by
CPI Group (UK) Ltd, Croydon, CR0 4YY

For all the Babys. Never stop trying.

Contents

Introduction

This is the book I have always wanted to write. I just hadn't realised it until 2019, the year of my fortieth birthday. My husband asked me what I wanted to do to mark the occasion, and I said without hesitation, 'I want to watch *Dirty Dancing*.' It even surprised me a little, hearing it come out of my mouth, but we sat down, found it on Netflix and settled in for the evening. I'm so glad we did, because it felt like coming home.

It had been some time since I'd last seen *Dirty Dancing* – a few years – but as soon we pressed play, and that banging, jangling opening to 'Big Girls Don't Cry' by The Four Seasons came through the speakers, I was right back there where it all began. I felt excited. I felt it wouldn't let me down, and I hoped I wouldn't regret it. I think in some ways I wanted to have a moment to reflect on the first 40 years of my life. To look back on my teenage years, and compare myself now, to the girl I was then. I needed a way to measure my progress, and with that need came the realisation that *Dirty Dancing* has been a constant influence in my life since I was 11 years old. Would my reaction to it remain the same? How much of that obsessed girl (because I was entirely obsessed with *Dirty Dancing*) remains within me, and how much of her has fallen away?

Of course, since my obsession abated from its height at around the age of 13 (when I was viewing it daily), I have watched *Dirty Dancing* a good few times, but as an adult I haven't really concentrated on it, or myself properly, as it plays out on the screen. Suddenly I wanted to focus on it, to really see it again in all its glory. I saw the fortieth birthday screening as part of my development as a person, and maybe a way of rounding off the first half of my life, giving me a pause as I enter the foothills of middle age, and beyond. This book is largely the product of that evening. I'm so glad my husband was cool with it.

And afterwards, as the credits rolled, I sat quietly by myself for a moment, enjoying that special glow you get when a story transports you. It's a 'proper film' – exciting, honest, sexy, moving, and uplifting. It was all still there. It's so life-affirming and joyful, but with enough substance to keep you satisfied. Life can wear you down, and by now I have suffered a few slings and arrows of my own, but I went to bed, newly 40 feeling as invincible as I had as a teenager. That night I fell in love with *Dirty Dancing* all over again.

But perhaps it's also been a while since you've seen it and are a little hazy yourself, or maybe you've never seen it at all (in which case, I'm somewhat amazed you are reading this book – you must really like me, thanks very much . . .), so here is a summary of *Dirty Dancing*, that I am going to write in a slight frenzy of love and excitement – can I get it all down in one attempt without checking anything? Let's go . . .

The Plot of Dirty Dancing

It's 1963 and Baby Houseman is 17 years old. As the film opens, she is sitting in the backseat of her family's car, as they drive to a holiday resort called Kellerman's in the Catskill Mountains. Baby is reading in the back, and somehow managing not to get car-sick. Her father Jake, a hard-working doctor, drives with a smile of contentment on his face, every inch the respectable family man. Her mother, Marge, is calm and understanding, while Lisa, Baby's older sister, panics that she hasn't brought enough shoes.

At first, the family settle into resort life, with its dancing lessons and boating lake. It's like a posh American Butlin's. It's relaxing, yes, but (dare Baby admit it?) perhaps a little boring. All this changes when professional dance instructors Penny and Johnny put on an evening show for the guests. Their performance is energetic, sexy and powerful, and Baby is transfixed, but also intrigued.

Later that night, she wanders into the staff area, though it's forbidden to guests. There, she finds Billy, a resort porter, who is attempting to carry three large watermelons to a party. Why he needs so many watermelons is not immediately clear, but not to worry, the point is that Baby loves to help out – she isn't just a spoilt rich girl – and so she takes one from him. She follows Billy into the party, and suddenly she is transported into a whole new world. A dirty, dirty world.

The hotel staff are unwinding after a hard day's work by having a good old dance. And it's not just any dancing – this is full-on, filthy grinding, a universe away from the sedate shuffling going on front of house. Penny and Johnny arrive, join in for a while, and then suddenly Baby is in Johnny's arms, having her first unofficial dancing lesson. This sensual moment reduces Baby to a puddle of lust, and will transform her jolly family holiday into an emotional, sexual and choreographically challenging few weeks that go on to change her life.

A couple of nights later, Baby is reluctantly hanging out with the hotel owner's grandson, smarmy Neil, who has taken a bit of a shine to her. By chance, she stumbles upon Penny, who is crying in a deserted kitchen. Baby runs to find Johnny, who comes to get his dance partner, and learns that Penny is pregnant by sleazy, spoilt waiter Robbie (who is by now romancing Baby's sister, Lisa). Billy has found a back-street abortionist who will take care of Penny's problem (it's 1963, and so there are very few safe options open to her), but it costs $250, which they don't have, and he is also only available on the night when Johnny and Penny have to perform a show dance at another hotel, the Sheldrake. Baby borrows the money from her father (without telling him what it's for) and also steps up to fill in for Penny on the night.

This means she must very quickly learn the dance, with Johnny as her teacher and partner. As they work together, we feel the tension building– both sexual and fearful – can she pull this off? Finally, they go off in Johnny's bashed-up old car to dance the mambo at the Sheldrake, while Billy takes Penny to have her pregnancy terminated. Apart from one small fluff on the dance floor, Baby gets through it. They are elated, but when they get back to Kellerman's late at night, they find Penny bleeding and in agony. The abortionist botched the job.

Baby runs to get her father, who treats and reassures Penny, but is horrified that Baby is hanging out with people he considers to be reckless and unreliable. He gets the wrong end of the stick and thinks Johnny is the father of Penny's baby, and is suspicious that he and Baby seem to know each other well. In his most 'upright and loving father' tone, he forbids her from having anything more to do with the dancers.

Baby defies her father, going straight to Johnny's cabin, where she asks him to dance. This becomes one of the greatest seduction scenes of all time. After some earth-shattering sex, they start a relationship. How could they not?

Meanwhile, a lonely older woman, Vivian, who has been paying Johnny for private dance lessons and anything else that 'comes up', discovers this new relationship, and in a fit of jealousy, accuses Johnny of stealing purses and wallets around various Catskills resorts. Max Kellerman tells the Housemans he is about to fire Johnny, and Baby has to step in and reveal – in front of everyone – that she has been spending her nights with him, as this is the only alibi he has to prove he is not the thief.

Later, it is revealed that an elderly couple, the Schumachers, are responsible for the thefts, but Kellerman fires Johnny anyway for his forbidden liaison with a guest, and so he leaves the resort and Baby with tears in his eyes. Eventually, everyone realises that Robbie was the one who got Penny pregnant, and Lisa breaks it off with him. There is a great deal of misery all round, and Baby has some home truths to tell her father about prejudice, and snobbery, and what it takes to be a decent person.

It seems the summer has come to a bad end, and not just for Baby, but for everyone. Is this the end of an era? A wider loss of innocence? Max Kellerman seems to think so, as he laments times gone by – are cosy family resorts which feature wig trying on sessions and ballroom dancing lessons going to survive? Are they simply too old-fashioned?

But what's this? It feels like the future has come to claim its place at the table. For at the evening talent show, on the last night of the season, Johnny Castle returns! Making a bombastic entrance, striding through the room for all the world like a man who hasn't just been fired, he finds Baby sitting with her parents in the audience. He takes her out of The Corner nobody should have put her in. They spontaneously perform their mambo routine so perfectly – including the impressive lift Baby couldn't manage at the Sheldrake (amazing what a life-changing shag can do for your confidence) – that everyone, even Max Kellerman and Baby's dad, agree they are perfect together, that Johnny is a good man, and Baby is her own woman. The whole audience are up and dancing and they all have the time of their lives.

And breathe. Well, I didn't check anything until after I'd finished. I just blurted it all out from memory. It was quite exciting, and hopefully, a helpful reminder as we take a deep dive into one of the greatest films of all time. Please do watch it though (who needs an excuse?), as it stands the test of time, and repeat viewings. It really is a phenomenal piece of work. Written by former dancer Eleanor Bergstein, drawing from her own life experience, filmed with a small budget ($4 million, which is nothing in feature film land) and a total lack of belief from the very studio that made it (they wanted it to go straight to VHS), it has grossed over $200 million worldwide, spawned multiple remakes, including a long-running live show, and thousands of articles, tribute events, wedding dances, proposals and even academic papers. It has also affected my life in the most unexpected ways.

Although I was not truly conscious of it until much later, in some respects *I Carried a Watermelon* cleverly started writing itself before I was even aware of my desire to explore and celebrate *Dirty Dancing* in real depth. A few years ago, I took part in a live show where the premise was you wrote a love letter to something very important to you, and then read it out for the audience. I chose *Dirty Dancing*, seemingly out of the blue, but once I started writing my letter I saw that I meant every word. I took it to the gig, stood up and delivered it, and I was amazed by the response. I thought people would simply laugh at me, but in fact I had a line of women, and some men, waiting afterwards to thank me, and hug me, and tell me how much it meant to them too. I looked for the letter when I started writing this book, and found it tucked away deep in my computer files. I read it again and still felt that burn of passion coming off the page. That letter became the start of this book.

What I began to realise, as I wrote my letter, was that *Dirty Dancing* has somehow shaped me and my choices, insinuating itself into my life in unexpected ways – it has shaped my sexual preferences, my attitudes to social class, good character, politics, love, relationships, casual sex, abortion, father/daughter issues and, of course, my understanding of whether it's possible to learn a complicated dance routine to perform in public in only a matter of days, at the same time as losing your virginity and ensuring an old, thieving couple is prosecuted for their crimes. All off the back of carrying a watermelon.

But why do I love *Dirty Dancing*? Would it be too much to say it's like the wind . . . through my tree? Yes, maybe, but it wouldn't be far off. It has everything – daughters and fathers, sisters, neglected wives, fear of how a pregnancy will affect your career, low-life scum and rich wankers, and how to handle them all. It's like an instruction manual for girls – well, middle-class girls anyway. Girls like me. 'Normal' girls who sometimes have a bit of a yen to get out there and do something a bit crazy. Nice girls who suddenly get an urge to carry a watermelon and get dirty with the 'wrong' sort of man.

I'm so glad *Dirty Dancing* got made, when it so nearly didn't – Eleanor Bergstein struggled to find funding for her script for years, and eventually had to shoot the whole thing over a few autumn weeks in a cold and rainy hotel resort in Virginia, on half the budget she had originally intended. I'm so glad it was released, when it so nearly wasn't – the company that stumped up the money couldn't initially see much potential beyond 'straight to video' and so it might have fallen by the wayside. And the fact that there is an abortion storyline right at its heart meant that it lost sponsorship money – but still Bergstein bravely resisted calls to change her film and remove the abortion. She was clear that we should not ever be complacent about our rights as women, and I think she has been proved 100 per cent correct in this regard.

I'm so happy that *Dirty Dancing* is now widely getting the more serious recognition it deserves, when it so easily may not have. It was dismissed for years as an enjoyable but largely insignificant piece of entertaining fluff – a commercial hit, yes, but nothing more – when in fact it is an important rite-of-passage story for girls. The female lead, Baby, is about as active in the story as it is possible to be. She makes it all happen. Every last moment is down to her, from the funding of an illegal abortion to the offer to fill in and learn the dance, to the extraordinary first seduction, and then the exoneration of Johnny as a thief. She drives the entire plot.

It has been much observed recently that things 'girls like' are often trivialised when compared to things 'boys like' – that stuff for women is romantic, domestic and ultimately insignificant, whereas stuff for men may be entertaining but also has 'universal themes' or an 'important message'. I can't think of another film I've seen that has more universal themes, or a more important message than *Dirty Dancing*. I'm so glad I've found this way of obsessing about it a little more, and a load of new people to do it with.

In its way, it is a feminist manifesto – a story with a heroine who has to defy her family, stand up for her principles, save the man she loves, and is finally lifted up in a floaty pink dress – you can still be a powerful woman in a floaty pink dress, after all. And you should never put up with being put in a corner, no matter how you're dressed. I'm glad it came into my life all those years ago, and I promise not to neglect it again. So, I'm wearing my Kellerman's t-shirt with pride (bought off the merchandise stand at the live show), even though it's slightly too small. That way, a little bit of it is always close to my heart, reminding me that nobody puts Baby in a corner. Thanks for being there, *Dirty Dancing* – I was a Baby when we met, but just look at me now.

1

Hungry Eyes

It was the summer of 1990, when everyone called me Katy and it never occurred to me to mind. Mainly because that was my name. I was 11 years old. The world felt new, my secondary school uniform felt newer, and as it was a weekend I was told that if I wanted to, I could stay up to watch this film I'd barely heard of on TV called *Dirty Dancing*.

I liked films with dancing in them – like *Bandwagon*, *Singin' in the Rain*, and *Top Hat*, with Gene Kelly or Fred Astaire. My favourite films were *Mary Poppins* and *The Sound of Music*, where women on a mission turn up and sort some people out. I liked the big numbers and sassy romantic story-lines, the up-against-the-clock drive when characters put their differences aside to pull together for the Big Show, the finale. I knew I liked the old stuff best. I could take or leave *Grease*, frankly – it's always struck me as a bit cold. Rizzo was all right, but Rizzo was meant to be a schoolkid and she looked like she was 45 and already on her third divorce. So even though this so-called *Dirty Dancing* was intriguing, I wasn't expecting much. I could always turn it off if I didn't like it.

Well.

I'm not sure I moved a muscle for the entire duration of the film. It's possible I held my breath. When it finished, I went straight upstairs for I couldn't bear to break the spell by talking to anyone. I lay in bed, staring at the glowing star stickers on my bedroom ceiling, tracing them from one to the next. I was trying to remember every moment and relive it. My body was alive with some unspecified but powerful energy. My mind was blown.

Scenes flew across my memory like shooting stars with such speed and brightness that I couldn't keep hold of them for long. It was a feeling. A heartbeat. And my heart was beating out of my chest. The opening – the family's arrival at the hotel – inauspicious in some respects, but with the promise of something more as porter Billy and Baby bond over unloading the bags. Then the tingle of the opening bars to '(I've Had) The Time of My Life', played slowly on the piano, a tease of the magic yet to come, as Baby makes her way up to the main house to 'look around', and later glimpses Johnny being told off by Max Kellerman ('no funny business, no conversation, and keep your HANDS OFF'). That opening dance number, where Penny and Johnny burst into the room and show what they can really do left me almost panting. The stage is set – this magnificent, talented man, pulsating with passion, but with a bad attitude, is breathing the same air as our Baby. The anticipation of what would happen next was almost too strong to handle . . .

And then, and then, oh and then that staff after-party – still my favourite scene – the sense of stepping into something ripe but forbidden, too good to turn back now. The dancing – like nothing I had ever seen before, raw and direct, primal. I felt hot thinking about it. And giggling and hugging myself over that line, 'I carried a watermelon', as Johnny curled his lip and Baby scolded herself for being so naff. I felt I could so easily be her. It was coming back to me in flashes – the impossibility of the task ahead of Baby – learning to dance to a professional standard in five days; the build-up of tension between Baby and Johnny, so perfectly paced – you knew what was going to happen, but you couldn't wait to see it – the delicious inevitability of it. And then that sex scene – the confidence of Baby now! To pull him in, to make it happen. Could a girl really do that? Could she just go and get a man if she wanted him? I couldn't believe it.

The twists and turns, the injustice of the stealing accusations against Johnny – I felt it burn within me, just like Baby did. She had to save him, I totally understood that – I would have done the same. The sick twist of heartbreak as he leaves her, the bleak wasteland that follows, as if life will never have colour again. And then the triumph of his return! He comes back! To find her! And to lift her high in the air, to show everybody what an amazing woman she has become. Oh god – I wanted to be Baby. I wanted it all to happen to me. I had to see it again. As soon as possible. I wanted this feeling to last forever.

But cruelly, the experience was fleeting and unrepeatable, it seemed. I had not thought to record the film off the telly as I watched it. I could not have foreseen the effect it would have on me, and now I was kicking myself. I didn't have the resources to video everything on the off-chance that it would radically re-order my emotions and inform my destiny. Nobody had that many blank videos at their disposal, surely – where would I store them, for god's sake? These were just some of the confused, racing thoughts zig-zagging through my overwhelmed and overheated brain. I couldn't believe I had lived before *Dirty Dancing*. I couldn't believe anything had mattered.

At first, I had to hold the memory of it within myself. I couldn't afford to buy it, and renting a video was an occasional treat, with the choice of film very much a committee decision involving the whole family, and I didn't detect quite the same level of enthusiasm in the house for *Dirty Dancing* that I was barely keeping under control. I had to wait.

Then, a few months later, I spotted it in the terrestrial TV schedule. The excitement was immense, and I made sure I was ready. I found a tape that had an episode of *Tomorrow's World* on it, followed by the second half of an old football match. They would be sacrificed in order that this might become The *Dirty Dancing* Tape. I carefully peeled back the old sticker, and replaced it with a brand new one, on which I wrote '*DIRTY DANCING* – DO NOT WIPE' in thick black ink. I crouched before the VCR player in readiness at the appointed time, lined it all up, and pressed record.

As soon as the film finished on TV, I immediately rewound the tape to check it. I pressed play. Please, please be there. It was. OK, for some reason, the first five minutes were missing, which was frustrating, but predictable considering our somewhat capricious video machine, which seemed to delight in mysteriously switching channels mid-record, or ending the recording early for no apparent reason, or just turning off altogether, so it had to be watched like a hawk. But the bulk of the film was there. I had done it, it was mine. IT WAS MINE. And nobody could take it away from me. I had caught the magic in a net.

So I watched it all over again. Twice in a night. It didn't feel excessive, it felt right. Because now it was available for me to view whenever I wanted to. And I wanted to. A lot. I watched *Dirty Dancing* after school. Every. Single. Day. For THREE MONTHS, until my concerned father confiscated and hid the tape, and it very much occurred to me to mind.

It took me a week to find it, discreetly rummaging in every drawer, ransacking then replacing the contents of various cupboards. I have always been an obsessive person – bloody-minded, stubborn, relentless in my pursuit of what I think should rightfully be mine. I am, to put it mildly, *tenacious*. I knew that the confiscated *Dirty Dancing* tape was somewhere in the house. I felt in my bones that my dad would not be so cruel, so callous as to throw it away entirely. I understood on some level that he was trying to save me from myself – perhaps encouraging me to widen my viewing habits. Or to do some homework. But life was different now that *Dirty Dancing* was in it. It was my lifeblood. I had to have it. It was my drug of choice. And so, I continued the search – of course I did.

And then, one night I got lucky – I had almost given up, but I had a hunch, and so I returned to a previously searched area. My diligence was rewarded. Pulling back an old garden chair, I gasped, and felt a quickening in my belly, as I caught sight of a familiar black plastic corner, tucked at the back of the junk cupboard under the stairs, behind a huge sack of dry dog food the dog wouldn't eat but my dad wouldn't throw away. Could it be? Could it really be? I reached into the cobwebby darkness, the musty, meaty, slightly sulphurous smell of old dog food wafting unnoticed into my nostrils. What did I care for that? I was holding *Dirty Dancing* in my hands again.

My elation is hard to describe. I had done it. I hadn't given up, and I had found it. The urge to watch it right there and then – to gorge on its sunlit perfection and wipe my chin afterwards – was strong but I had to bide my time: it was past 11pm when I made my glorious discovery, and though the house was quiet, I couldn't risk being caught. Trembling, I forced myself to place the precious tape back in its meaty-smelling hiding place, kissing it first, and went back to bed quivering with anticipation. Within a few hours, I would be watching *Dirty Dancing* again.

By now I was 12, and allowed to be at home alone after school until my parents finished work. Tomorrow would be just such a day. Tomorrow, and tomorrow, and tomorrow. Such sweet joy tomorrow would bring. I would arrive home from school at 4.15pm. My parents would usually arrive around 6pm. That was my window. I needed 1 hour, 46 minutes to watch the whole thing, which was tight, but if I fast-forwarded through the opening credits, I could do it all, rewind it, and have it safely back behind the bag of dog food before anyone knew what had happened.

I barely slept. I couldn't concentrate at school. Baby, and Johnny, and Penny, and all the others were waiting for me. I crashed through the door, dumped my bag, and breathlessly retrieved the one and only copy of *Dirty Dancing* I could ever hope to possess (videos were bloody expensive in those days). I put it on. I pressed play. I licked my lips and sat down on the sofa. I was ready. It began.

Oh my god, every minute was still perfect. I sunk into it, let it envelope me. I felt safe but also excited. Perhaps this is what love feels like, I thought. As the film ended I once again felt that heady sense of being invincible. I could do anything. I was just like Baby, and there was a Johnny out there for me somewhere.

Until one day – disaster! The tape broke, and it stuck at the point where Johnny defiantly says, 'You just put your pickle on everybody's plate, college boy . . .' and would not move on from there, no matter how many times I ejected the tape and wound it on manually with a coin. I tried to move it the other way, thinking I could get beyond the glitch. It seemed to work for a moment – I could feel the tape spooling on nicely, but then there was an ominous clicking sound, and peering inside the black box, I could see it was now hopelessly tangled. Oh god. OH GOD.

I held the VHS tape limply in my hands like a beloved deceased hamster. Should I bury it? With a full service? I couldn't believe it. It was gone. A piece of me went with it – partly because I loved *Dirty Dancing* so much, and partly because I had ripped my nail trying to fix the tape, and the torn part had dropped inside.

I filled the vacuum as best I could. There was no internet at this stage, of course, or maybe there was, but it was of no use to me as it merely connected a few military bases, American universities, and a clutch of badly-dressed geniuses in garages sending each other strings of numbers that meant nothing. So I survived by being creative – I found coping strategies to keep it alive within me. I forced my best friend from school to allow me to act out my favourite scenes in my living room. (I should clarify here, it was the dancing scenes I wanted, specifically the tuition scenes – I did not wish to recreate anything sexual with my best friend, though she may have been more nervous of where this was heading than she let on.) I co-opted my little sister into the game whenever I could. She was up for it, being a fan herself, but I always took it too far, until people were broken.

I had of course made a taped copy of the full soundtrack, which I had borrowed from the library. God, how I loved those songs; they introduced me to a whole new genre of music. 'Hungry Eyes' by Eric Carmen still makes my heart flutter, and the stomach-drop of pain you feel as Solomon Burke sings 'Cry to Me' hits me every time. 'In the Still of the Night' by Fred Parris and The Satins is a crooning delight. I had never heard songs like this before, and they excited me. Not to mention '(I've Had) the Time of My Life', with that immensely distinctive half-time chorus opener, which then picks up a nice little groove you can't help but move to.

And then there is the also wonderful but slightly less acknowledged second soundtrack, which features some of the more obscure Latin dance tracks, for the true enthusiast – I had to order it specifically from the library, and I made a tape of that too. I had all the dances tracks at my disposal now, and I used them to the point of wearing them, and myself out. All day at school, I would badger my best friend to come over, and when she relented, we would do the 'Hungry Eyes' rehearsal montage with Penny over, and over again (oh, how I wanted a red leotard with a little gold belt, and black fishnet tights, and gold sandals), with her standing in front of me, 'teaching' her the moves. I was too bossy to be Baby – I had to be Penny. For some reason, I always loved that whole sequence, starting with Penny looking at Johnny with great meaning over Baby's head – this is the moment where we see how high the stakes are for them. This has to work, it just has to.

My best friend, though, was soon fed up with her role. She liked *Dirty Dancing* well enough, but I managed to eclipse her with my obsessive behaviour – I took it to an unnecessary level. I wanted it all the time, to the exclusion of all else. Finally, when pushed to the limit of her tolerance and Latin dance abilities, she refused to participate any longer. Or even come to my house for fear of an ambush. My sister also had other interests to attend to. And so, now I was alone with my madness.

My requests for a new shop-bought copy of the *Dirty Dancing* video, with a real cover and everything, to replace the mangled tape, for my birthday, and then at Christmas fell on deaf ears – clearly an enforced separation was now underway and probably for my own good. *Dirty Dancing* was again forbidden, and we all know how effective that is when keeping teenage girls from the object of our desires.

Dirty Dancing was my unsuitable first boyfriend, my leather jacket relationship, my staff-guest liaison, and my parents were stepping in to preserve my honour. I wouldn't have access to my own copy again for another seven years.

Of course, tape or no tape, the film still influenced my real-life crushes. I ought to confess at this point that, until the moment Johnny Castle came into my life, my first real love was Michael Jackson. This was the late 1980s, and though people thought he was weird, there was not yet any hint of the full horror that was to come. I wrote him long, long letters. I read *Moonwalk* – the official biography – several dozen times. I even tried to 'trick' International Directory Enquiries into giving me his phone number by calling 151 from the phone box at Amersham station on my way home from school, and saying as convincingly as I could that 'a man named Michael Jackson has called and left no number – I believe his address is Neverland Valley Ranch, Santa Barbara, California, USA', and then waited patiently as they confirmed what I had deep down suspected but could not bring myself to admit – that the number was, indeed, listed as 'ex-directory'. True story.

Johnny represented a new kind of man for me – unequivocally heterosexual in an old-fashioned 'movie star male lead' kind of way: tough, strong, emotionally closed, waiting for the touch of a good woman to open him up. I'd seen them on film before, but they were usually either cowboys or played by Tom Cruise. Johnny had old school sex appeal, he had swagger, he had improbably 1980s clothes and musical tastes, given that he lived in 1963. He was wary and cautious to begin with – a man of few words – but then once you got to know him, he opened like a flower. He had vulnerabilities, he had talent, he had the moves. And he was clearly very, very good at sex.

This was all very well, but it had to remain in the realms of fantasy, because as I looked around me, there seemed to be few men of my age (12) that could really match up. The boys at my school were perfectly fine, if you liked competitions to see how long you could hold your hand over a Bunsen flame without crying, extended belching displays where we had to also 'smell the burp', and having your burgeoning breasts commented on at every possible opportunity. But Johnny was a 'real man', to use a now outdated and probably somewhat toxic phrase. I was done with studied ambiguity – I wanted a hunk. Narrow-hipped, long-haired, feminine-featured men with a suggestion of eye-liner were no longer my bag. Nothing wrong with them, but they did not push my buttons. I wanted someone who hid their sensitivities under a gruff exterior. I wanted someone who might throw a punch under certain circumstances, especially if some 'Robbie the Creep' type was to impugn my honour. I wanted a project. Just like Baby, I wanted to sort someone out. I wanted a diamond in the rough.

But this was a side issue. As I look back, I can now see that while Johnny Castle was a formative type for me when it came to men, my real crush was on Baby. It was all about Baby. She was called Frances; my middle name is Frances. And the similarities didn't end there – o-ho no. We both had a fire in our bellies for social justice and human rights – she was joining the Peace Corps; I did a 24-hour sponsored silence in aid of Oxfam (much welcomed it seemed at the time, by parents and teachers alike . . . in fact, there were enquiries as to whether, in return for a larger donation, the period of silence could be extended). She liked wearing cut-off denim shorts, I liked wearing cut-off denim shorts. Mine were home-made though, and a little less 'neat' than Baby's.

In fact, I had gone a bit nuts with the scissors one day and hacked up my best jeans, cutting each leg from the knee into a long, jagged point that each reached to mid-calf. My horrified grandmother, who was looking after me and my sister that afternoon, could only look on and whisper, 'Are you sure you're allowed to do that to your clothes, Katy . . .?' The reflection in the mirror when wearing them made my actions instantly regrettable, although I felt I had to style it out to save face in front of Grandma. Frankly, I looked like an extra from *Oliver!*, but nonetheless I wore them stubbornly to the park and library that day, and tried to look nonchalant and vaguely superior to anyone I caught sniggering.

That night, I cut the jagged pieces off, creating a wonky and uneven but more traditional denim short, and then stuffed them in a drawer and pretended to my parents I didn't know where they were. They never saw the light of day again (the jeans, not my parents). How I coveted Baby's beautiful pair, with their perfect turn-ups and smoothly flattering cut through the hips. The dream pair of denim shorts still eludes me to this day, but I will never stop looking.

Besides my clothes, I tried to get *Dirty Dancing* into my life in any way I could. I begged and pleaded to go on a family holiday to a resort, in the Catskills, where I now knew through painstaking research (again, pre-internet – I had to actually ask things, of actual humans standing in front of me. Can you imagine? The horror) was the area in upstate New York known for its holiday resorts where the fictional Kellerman's nestled. It was made very clear to me that I might as well ask for the moon on a stick, because flying from London to the US to an all-inclusive resort for three weeks for a family of four was (a) prohibitively expensive, and (b) wouldn't happen even if we won a million pounds, as the idea of going for enforced cha-cha lessons and group aerobics sessions in the lake with a bunch of strangers was really considered a kind of hell in our household.

So it was a campsite in Cornwall again, like last year, and the year before. And don't get me wrong, these were enjoyable holidays full of freedom, clear waters, hot sand and thick clotted cream, but with the best will in the world, it was not Kellerman's. And I wanted Kellerman's, badly. It wasn't that I thought I would somehow actually find Baby and Johnny, and Billy and Penny, and carry a watermelon and have to dance at the Sheldrake at incredibly short notice. I wasn't completely insane. But I wanted my own Baby experience, and to do that, there must be staff, and an element of 'backstage' to stumble in on. There needed to be staff quarters to be caught in. There had to be some rules for me to disobey, and someone to compromise my reputation with. And although there was a jolly old Cornish couple who ran the campsite shop, and a guy 'on reception' who honestly looked like a retired pirate, who could perhaps be termed 'staff', they didn't live onsite, and even if they did, the chances of me coming across the three of them engaged in some sort of sweat-laced-dance-off-cum-orgy in the early hours seemed slim, though perhaps I underestimate them.

It was mostly roaming the ancient, pagan Cornish landscape for me, trying to find other children who would willingly participate in spontaneous, free-style dance lessons. It was fun, but not satisfactory. I had a longing for romance and drama, and something magical to happen by moonlight. And one year, as unlikely as it sounds, I got it.

We visited the Minack Theatre to see a production of *Guys and Dolls*. It is a spectacular outdoor auditorium, cut right into the rocky cliffs, where the audience sits on smooth stone benches and the performers play in front of the backdrop of the Atlantic Ocean. On a clear night at the right time of year, halfway through the show the sun sets and the moon rises, glittering on the water, kissing everyone with a pale silver. This was just such a night. And even better, we were staying over that day with a school friend of mine and her family in a large cottage right next to the theatre itself.

The show was so beautiful that afterwards I floated back to the house in the dusky light, my head full of songs and a new crush on my hands: Sky Masterson. I was not being disloyal, I told myself, for this was surely only a holiday romance, and Johnny was where my heart lived. But Johnny was at home.

My friend and I were sharing a room. We sat on the wide window seat with the old wooden sash frame pulled up high, so the warm night air would envelop us and we could hear the sea. We wanted to keep the feeling going for as long as we could. And then we heard it – singing, men singing, the sound will-o'-the-wisping to us across the twilight. They were cast members, singing songs from the show.

We froze on the window seat – this was the dream. Was it in fact, a dream? The bedroom overlooked the garden, with a path that wound its way down to a low stone wall and an iron gate at the end. Two men were now silhouetted against the full moon, the shapes of their costumes – sharp suits and trilby hats – clear against the pale brightness. They stopped at the end of the garden, and looked towards us. Straight at us. We ourselves were picked out by the low glow of a night light inside, behind us. There was a pause. We held our breath. And then they started singing again, this time just for us, songs from the show: a medley.

This was it. It was happening. This was as close to backstage at Kellerman's as I was going to get on England's most westerly point. In fact, across the now near invisible horizon, lay Kellerman's itself, just 3,000 miles away as the crow flies. It was enough. I was transfixed. I wondered if we should steal out of the house, trip down the path, and try to inveigle ourselves with these men, perhaps there would be a cast party somewhere, perhaps there would be dancing, perhaps there would be a call for me to step in on stage to cover a cast member who needed time off for a tricky personal medical procedure that had to be kept hush-hush, perhaps, perhaps, perhaps . . . But then the singing stopped, the men waved to us and moved on, their crisp outlines smudging into the night.

We had been, and there is simply no other word for it, *serenaded*. SERENADED, for god's sake. For the rest of the holiday, I would lie on my inflatable mattress in our canvas tent, listening to the August rain and trying not to touch the sides, feeling all my feelings. It was the same feeling as I got when I watched *Dirty Dancing* – a tingle of magic, the sense of a million possibilities glittering before me.

The next obvious step in my obsession was to enrol in some actual dance classes. A short distance away from home, in the next town, there was a small dance school, which offered lessons in ballet, tap, modern, and something called 'national', which was basically learning the national dances of the various countries of the world – a singularly useless skill, but undeniably good exercise. I was naturally disappointed to find that the merengue, the salsa and the mambo were not on offer, but I made do. It was a start. After all, this was the

Home Counties – Latin dance was really not a thing. But I did all of it, even the national dancing – all day Saturday, and Wednesday nights. And I loved it.

It may not come as a huge shock to learn that I was not deemed physically suitable for an internationally successful career as a prima ballerina, but I could definitely do modern or jazz dance pretty well, and tap too. I could *feeeel* the music. G-gong. G-gong. I could move to it naturally, instinctively. I felt that if I had to step in at any point to help a dancer in anguish, and thereby meet the love of my life, I would be OK. I would do Johnny proud, and we would then have excellent sex. I was prepared.

Our dance teacher wasn't Penny by any stretch of the imagination, but she taught us the basics and was mostly encouraging in a terrifying kind of way. And she certainly made no secret of her opinions on our figures. On one occasion, she burst into the cramped changing room during our lunch break to find us all eating various bars of chocolate. Her face reddened in disgust, and she jabbed a finger at each of us in turn, punctuating her warning that, 'They. Will. Make. You. Fat.' A jab for each of us. I was munching a Bounty in a particularly bovine way at the time, and her unexpected accusation landed heavily. I suddenly felt ashamed and guilty. I finished the Bounty though. I wasn't about to waste it.

Each year my dance school would host a local show called 'the Choreographic' and we pupils would have the opportunity to design our own routines and perform them for members of the public. There would be prizes and cups, and one horrifying event where we would have to spontaneously choreograph and perform a three-minute dance, onstage, to a piece of music we had never heard before. The risk of humiliation was high, and failure almost certain, and it was the only compulsory category. Whether it was meant to be enjoyable, or simply an expression of our dance teacher's sadistic streak we will never know, but it scared the living shit out of everyone. Everyone except me. Because I was prepared.

By this point, dance improvisation was basically my hobby. At home, at the weekend, I would wait for everyone to leave the house, on errands or trips out, and beg to stay behind so I could play music as loudly as I was able on our HiFi stack and choreograph my own routines. I use the term 'choreograph' lightly – it was more a case of me just flinging myself about as wildly as I could, having cleared the furniture to make an acceptable dance space. It was absolute primeval abandon. A casual passing observer, catching the display through a window, might even be alarmed. But god, it felt good. It was total release, and I felt connected to *Dirty Dancing* through it. I felt I understood what made those characters tick. I felt part of their world. I was *Dirty Dancing*. And incredibly, that year, I won the Improvisation Cup at the Choreographic. This was mainly down to the fact that I had managed (by chance) to strike a pose right at the very moment the music stopped, which was accidental but impressive, since we had never heard it before. But it was also because of *Dirty Dancing* – it had made me bolder, braver. So, when the music started, I just danced, and I didn't care about anything else.

The white heat of my besotted first encounter with the film began to fade when I was around 13. It had lasted two years – longer than some marriages – and I think made a foundation stone for the rest of my life. My obsessive tendencies were unexpectedly transferred around this age when I quite suddenly became a fundamentalist evangelical Christian, which lasted until I lost my faith at 19, after starting a theology degree.

I would like to say that I fell in love with Jesus, but if I'm honest, I fell in love with the worship band leader at my church. I managed to get myself into the band so I could moon at him from close quarters, though my love was firmly unrequited. Frankly, Jesus barely got a look in. I was 'with the band'. Finally, I had made it backstage, where I liked to be, and still do. *Dirty Dancing* had given every backstage area a romantic flavour for me – the glamour, the secrets. And the band leader was a man of few words, a little gruff, but with his own damage and vulnerabilities. He was talented, but had seen a lot of trouble. His family life was tough. I think you know where I'm going with this . . .

Yes, *Dirty Dancing* has provided the template for my emotional life, my romantic life, my sex life and even my marriage. It inspired a love of dancing that has continued to this day: for better, for worse. It was like having a cool older sister, or a glamorous but slightly drunk auntie who will tell you a bit about life – about men and women, and the way we lock together, and then twirl apart. It showed me what it felt like to be a teenage girl, and how you become a woman. It goes beyond my experience, and has affected so many like me, and unlike me.

And of course, it gave us all something to say whenever we are stuck for words: 'I carried a watermelon.' So many people have now told me they've gasped 'I carried a watermelon' in an awkward moment just to ease the tension. Those four words have now entered the mainstream lexicon. It's a phrase that has influenced our culture – you can buy (and I have) t-shirts, mugs, water bottles and more with it printed on. It's even the title of a book . . . This is a huge achievement for any writer, so congratulations to Eleanor Bergstein – there aren't many who can boast that four words conjured from their own imagination would become a phrase known and loved by so many people. But there's so much more to say. Follow me . . .

2
Do You Love Me?

*B*aby Houseman loses her virginity twice on screen, and the first time is through the medium of dance. The moment she wangles her way into the staff party with the infamous watermelon is where her sexual odyssey really kicks off. In the next 90 minutes or so, we discover that *Dirty Dancing* has an awful lot to say about sex, youth and freedom – much of which is extremely helpful to a young girl watching, with her eyes out on stalks.

Johnny Castle approaches Baby as she stands awkwardly in the corner, seeming gruff and unimpressed at first that his cousin Billy has smuggled in a 'guest daughter' – as we have already learnt, due to excellent exposition, proprietor Max Kellerman does not approve of extra-curricular staff-guest fraternising, at least not for the dancers, so Johnny is understandably concerned that this intruder may get them all in trouble.

Baby is already slightly turned on by the deeply filthy dance displays going on all around her. As she follows Billy through the steaming, writhing mass, her skin flushes and her lips part. She looks a bit 'glowy', shall we say. But that's nothing compared with what's in store for her sharp sexual trajectory. Because Johnny Castle casts off his initial wariness and gets the devil in him for a moment. He invites Baby to dance. And so, it begins . . .

Using dance as a proxy for sex isn't new. In fact, using anything as a proxy for sex is fairly standard across all art forms – cutting to fountains gushing, or the tide rushing in at the crucial moment, is now so clichéd that it's a joke in itself. Even Jane Austen was at it in *Pride and Prejudice*, when she used Elizabeth Bennet's carefree lone muddy walks, her flushed cheeks and bright eyes shining from the fresh air, to convey a kind of vigorous drive and lust for life that does the job for Mr Darcy. But here in *Dirty Dancing*, the metaphorical shield is Durex-thin – it is in fact quite explicit. Basically, dancing = sex with your jeans on.

The scene continues, with Baby joining the throng at Johnny's invitation. As the more experienced dancer, he calms Baby down, gets her to feel the rhythm, and she stiffly lurches and thrusts with all the style and grace of Theresa May at a hip hop night, and as you watch, you feel the cringe go deep on her behalf.

But he doesn't laugh at her, or belittle her. As Otis Redding belts out 'Love Man', he pulls her to him, tells her to look in his eyes, to relax her shoulders, and – what do you know? – within minutes they have locked groins and she has become like a cooked noodle in his arms. The song ends, and he leaves her, but she can barely stand up. She appears to be melting from the vagina outwards. The message is this: a good dance will prepare you for good sex. You need not fear losing your virginity with a man who dances like this. It won't even hurt, for god's sake – you'll be so ready for it, you'll have excess natural lubricant to bottle and sell.

I don't need to be the latest person to describe the awkwardness of watching sex scenes with your parents – there are a million comedy routines covering it, and we all know what that's like in any case from sphincter-tightening first-hand experience. And so yes, on my first viewing there was all the usual 'eyes-straight-ahead-don't-swallow-don't breathe' stuff going on, which meant my enjoyment was a bit . . . subdued.

Part of the sex appeal is how imperfect some of them look at times, by modern film standards. It's not all painted and pretty; it's sweaty and lusty, with mascara running down their cheeks with the sheer heat of it all. I remember being absolutely thrilled with it – not necessarily in an explicitly erotic way, but it certainly gave me a feeling of warm excitement. It all looked so physical and immediate – you can feel the chemistry coming off the screen. Sex is natural and easy. Bodies are fun and sensual. So, feel good about yourself. And I did, after watching it.

So, while dancing is obviously the main focus of the film, and the dancers set the tone in a smoky, oily kind of way, it's sex that really underpins the whole thing. In her review of *Dirty Dancing* when it first came out in 1987, the eminent American film critic Pauline Kael wrote in the

New Yorker, 'dancing is a transparent metaphor for main character Baby's sexual initiation . . . this is a girl's coming of age fantasy: through dancing she ascends to spiritual and sensual perfection.'

Ascending to spiritual and sensual perfection sounds pretty good to me now as a 40-year-old woman, never mind as a teenager, but as a young girl approaching puberty the thought of sex terrified and fascinated me in equal measure. I had a habit of trying to get boys' attention, but as soon as they showed any interest, I would feel sick and back off hard. Of course, I was still too young to actually do it, or really want to do it, but trying out your powers early on the opposite sex, with varying degrees of success, seems to be a rite of passage for many girls.

My attempts were clumsy to say the least. I was not in any way coquettish or even especially nice, and thought being sarcastic was highly seductive. If I fancied someone a bit, I would relentlessly take the piss until there could be no doubt that I considered them scum of the earth. It was counterproductive, but kept me and my delicate feelings protected in public. 'You'll cut yourself on that tongue one day,' a teacher said to me after overhearing a conversation I was having with one poor victim.

The idea of flirting, or being soft in any way, made me feel ill. I can't explain why, but it was a physical sensation – a visceral recoil. Thankfully, I got over it, so perhaps it was just nerves, but for a long time my relationships were always verbally combative – I saw it as a sign of affection, or rather, the kind of affection I was willing to express at the time. The idea that you should be nice to boys if you want them to like you seemed perfectly logical to me, it was just when it came to anything romantic that I went a bit strange. I had lots of friends who were boys, and they had always seemed fairly interchangeable with the girls. I didn't wear dresses much, or skirts. I liked blue jeans, blue t-shirts and scruffy trainers. I mostly had my hair short, and could barely be bothered to brush it. If I dressed up at all, it was leggings and a large jumper. Before I watched *Dirty Dancing* that first time, I don't think I really understood intimacy between couples, and the kind of 'sex appeal' that was usually shown in films felt like it came from another planet. I couldn't relate at all.

But now here was a girl called Baby, who wore jeans and white plimsolls, and denim shorts, and loose-fitting t-shirts, who was slightly awkward and bad-tempered with this man, Johnny, and yet he seemed to like it. Here was a girl like me, wearing clothes like mine (only better), having her first sexual relationship with a man who clearly knew his way around. She didn't wear make-up, she didn't have a push-up bra, she didn't stick her bum out, or pretend to be weak in his presence. She didn't use any tricks. She was wholly and completely herself, authentic in all respects, even as she changed her entire world view in the space of three weeks. And, as a result, she had the shag of her life. In fact, read 'Time of My Life' as 'Shag of My Life' and you get quite an accurate sense of the journey of the film – perhaps that was Eleanor Bergstein's euphemistic intention all along.

I believe this formed the basis for how I approached the notion of sex appeal as I entered my teens for real. I knew

I wasn't pretty in the sense of 'pretty-pretty' – I knew who those girls were and what you were supposed to look like to be one of them, but I didn't really try to be like them. I still don't most of the time. I have learnt through my professional work that if you want to look properly good, or as good as you can possibly look, you need a minimum of two hours with a professional hair and make-up artist, seriously restrictive undergarments (or 'shapewear' as it is coyly known) and a four-inch heel or higher. I'd rather be comfortable. I'd rather look slightly shit, smile for the picture, resolve never ever to look at it, and then enjoy the rest of the evening. I even applied this to my own wedding, which is why we didn't have a professional photographer. I don't regret it – I had the best time. I wore a blue dress because I always manage to spill my food, I partook eagerly of the hog roast and pavlova, and then danced all night.

Penny – played by eighties pin-up Cynthia Rhodes – Johnny's dance partner, drips old-school glamour and always looks astonishing. Tiny Jennifer Grey looks positively dumpy next to her sometimes, but it doesn't matter. Because it doesn't matter to Baby, and it certainly doesn't matter to Johnny. Late in the film, Baby's more groomed older sister Lisa offers to do her hair, but then stops herself with the line, 'No, you're pretty in your own way.'

'Pretty in your own way' became my lifeline. My mantra. There is one brief scene in *Dirty Dancing* where Baby tries to change herself or her appearance for Johnny, and that is when she stops on the stone steps to apply her sister's 'beige irides-cent lipstick', swiped from her drawer in the family cabin. And even then she makes a bit of a joke about it, draping herself over a railing in a cartoonish mockery of how a Hollywood siren might move. She's having fun, and to be honest, that lipstick would be so plain it would barely register. The only other time she makes an effort is when she dances with Johnny at the Sheldrake, and that is for professional reasons. Yes, her outfits get sexier and skimpier as she learns to dance, but this does not appear calculated to have a sexual pull on Johnny, more for us to see that she is gaining confidence in her own body as she learns what it can do.

Other than these moments, it's 'pretty in your own way' the whole time. I still look at myself in the mirror, and I see the imperfections, and then I catch myself and murmur comfortingly, 'You're pretty in your own way.' This is partly to excuse the sheer lack of effort on my part on a day-to-day basis, but also it's a kind, realistic and affirming little ritual that makes you forget the pressures of having to contour yourself until you basically resemble a Kardashian, no matter the original shape of your features.

In fact, there is never any suggestion that Baby has to achieve a certain 'look' to get Johnny's attention, or win his desire. The first time they have sex, it follows the car journey back from the Sheldrake, in which Baby climbs in the back seat to change out of her more glamorous and revealing dancing outfit and back into the jeans and shirt she was wearing before. Johnny seems genuinely attracted by her character, her commitment, her goodness and her determination. That is what turns him on. However you look at it, this is a great message for a young girl entering the world of sexual politics for the first time. Or anyone, in fact.

There are no games with Baby and Johnny, and when you think about it, that is quite striking. They work together, they fancy each other, so they fuck. They communicate directly with each other. They don't send messages through friends, or play hard to get. They want it, so they do it. And then they do it again, and again, and again. The central issue of the film is not whether she has slept with him too fast to retain his respect, or whether he fancies someone else more, or whether she's cool enough for him. It's whether or not she can solve the mystery of a series of purse thefts from the hotel for which he is accused before he is fired. And whether she can respect herself, even when she loses the respect of her father. It's strong stuff. And it's all very sexy, especially when they keep dancing with each other half-naked and a bit sweaty.

Even when they think they are going to have to separate for good, there is very little angst or stress. Watching this scene now, it is incredible to me how mature it is. Standing opposite each other next to his car on a dusty track, they embrace. He says, 'I'll never be sorry,' she agrees, and then he drives away. She waves for a moment, pauses and then turns to walk back to the hotel. It's so weirdly calm. They both seem to accept that it was fun while it lasted, they had some good times, but now it's over, and they have to go their separate ways. There is no suggestion that Baby will throw away her future for him, or that he will pursue her, or let her down at a later date. They kiss, they hug, he drives off, and she waves. And all the while 'She's Like the Wind', composed and performed by Swayze himself, plays over the top. What's not to love? When you compare it to the hysterical, 'my life is over' form of comparable scenes in more recent romantic dramas, it's revolutionary. It basically tells you that you can have a holiday romance, and then get over it and get on with your life. Think how many wasted hours we could all have saved over the years, when we've agreed to meet up with a holiday shag back home, and then sat opposite each other in a dreary pub, wondering, faintly embarrassed, what the hell you ever saw in each other, praying no one you know comes in.

But even though I had all this formative education thanks to *Dirty Dancing*, my teenage years were barren, sexually speaking. In fact, I think you could even throw the word 'frigid' around and I wouldn't kick you in the nuts. Of course, there's nothing wrong with not being ready, but I was definitely resisting even the most innocent of romantic encounters – a light touch, a gentle snog. I think now that part of the attraction of becoming a full-on, fundamentalist, evangelical Christian from the age of 13 to 19 was the fact that they didn't believe in sex before marriage, so I always had an excuse. 'I can't have sex with you because of Jesus,' is a very effective deterrent, if you didn't already know . . .

I somehow knew that the reality would be a let-down, compared with Baby's first experience, and therefore also the version I'd imagined for myself. My fear was in fact confirmed by my first snog, back at that Cornish campsite, at the age of 13. I remember his tongue thrusting in and out of my mouth with such vigour that I wondered whether he was trying to eat my dinner. Of course, he was young too – no doubt he is now a top-level snogger – but this put me off for a long time. It felt nothing like the soft kisses that Baby and Johnny share. But nevertheless, there was a dusky magic to it, and that moment just before the moment, when you know it's going to happen and something inside takes over, is still a thrilling memory. That feeling of stepping outside to share a cigarette with someone you fancy, and realising they fancy you too, and it's going to happen, and it's going to happen now, is one of the most delicious sensations known to mankind.

Deep down I was waiting for Johnny Castle. An older man, perhaps. Or at least someone who knew what to do. In the film, he is meant to be 25 to Baby's 17, and Swayze himself was 34 when it was made (Grey was 27). This keeps us just on the right side of 'slightly pervy', but the age gap, both real and imagined, has been remarked upon before. It is really the sincerity and innocence of the performances that keeps us from any true discomfort.

Some have said maybe Johnny does this every year, and Baby is simply his latest victim, but I'm not having that. Because there is nothing untoward or unequal about the sex Baby and Johnny have. In fact, Swayze himself understood this, saying in a TV profile of his life and career that the film shows the loss of Baby's innocence, but the regaining of Johnny's. A more beautiful and insightful comment on their respective journeys, I could not compose.

And when that astonishing sex scene finally happens, crucially, it is Baby who initiates it. She seduces Johnny. She comes to his cabin, expressly disobeying her father, who has literally just told her she is to have nothing more to do with him. She's performed her duties at the Sheldrake, so there is no need for her to come at all. Baby may hope to use apologising to Johnny for her father's behaviour as a cover for her late-night visit, but she knows perfectly well what she's really after, and suggests they dance together, one last time. As they move to the cracked soul of 'Cry to Me' by Solomon Burke, she runs her hands over his naked torso and grips hold of his buttock like a woman who knows exactly what she wants. It is one of the sexiest scenes of all time. Watching them blend together, in and out of bed, is enough to give you palpitations. And the best thing about it all is that Baby clearly loves it – she is not ashamed or guilty, she just wants more. Here is a teenage girl losing her virginity with no misery, shame or tears. She loves sex. It can be done!

When you are brought up with the constant reinforcement that your virginity is both a hindrance and a prize, that the losing of it will be traumatic no matter how you do it, can you conceive of how astonishing this film is? Let's stand back and give it a moment. Let's applaud it. Teenage girls can love sex and not be 'little minxes' or 'sluts'. Who knew? I want more of this.

I wrote a play in 2018 called *3 Women*, with an 18-year-old girl in it, and I wanted the same for her. Writing her dialogue, when she's talking about how much she loves sex, was such a thrill. I thought of Baby throughout. When she shouts that immortal line to Johnny as they argue about their fate – 'Most of all, I'm scared of leaving this room and never feeling again, my whole life, the way I feel when I'm with you' – I think I knew, even as a young girl, that she meant sex – there's unfinished business here, and Baby could surely sense it was building to something wonderful. It's a cry of lust, as much as it is one of love.

Johnny clearly has no idea of the sheer power he possesses here. He blinks back at her, bewildered. But he has had this effect on women before, so it shouldn't come as too much of a surprise, though it's sort of sweet that he hasn't realised. And it can get him in trouble – one woman who has experienced his skills, Vivian, is even prepared to tell an absolute stonking lie because she fears she will never get near it again.

Ah yes, Vivian. Vivian Pressman, brilliantly and subtly played by Miranda Garrison (although on first viewing I was convinced it was British actress Lesley Joseph, of *Birds of a Feather* fame . . .), brings us to a different kind of sex represented in *Dirty Dancing*. In fact, there's a lot of shagging in *Dirty Dancing*. It drives the plot as much as the dancing does. And a lot of general sexiness – everyone looks pretty up for it all the time. Even Baby's parents, Jake and Marge Houseman, have a naughty twinkle in their eyes, to be frank.

The air of melancholy and loneliness, and faded glamour Vivian brings can be lost in the frenzy of the first few viewings, but it's there and it's important. When I first watched it, I was too overwhelmed by it all to really take her, and her storyline, in. But later in life I have grown quite fascinated by it.

It's Max Kellerman's introduction to Vivian early in the film that sets the tone. He watches her gracefully dancing with Johnny, a wry and sympathetic smile on his face as he explains to the Housemans that she is a 'bungalow bunny' – women who spend all week alone at Kellerman's while their wealthy husbands work, arriving at the weekend only to ignore them further, choosing to play cards instead of dancing with their wives. It is clear that Vivian and Johnny have some form of quiet arrangement, and that she is one of the women 'stuffing diamonds in his pockets' that he refers to later in his speech to Baby about his experience of being sexually exploited in the resort. There are no sniggers, or jibes about older women. He doesn't suggest that he is lowering himself, or is repulsed by her. There is an implied competition with Baby of course, which Baby wins, and yes, her youth is part of it, but also there is a sense that Vivian represents a jaded, toxic scene that we wish Johnny was not involved with, and Baby is his route out.

My only criticism of this storyline is that, as I have got older, I have wished to learn more about Vivian. There's so clearly a real story there, and she would have things to say about life, men, and probably a whole lot else. Probably more than Marge Houseman, who doesn't seem to have a lot going on, and even less to contribute, save for her final bark at her husband, 'Sit down, Jake', as Baby and Johnny take to the stage in front of everyone.

It took me a while to realise what was going on in one of the final scenes, where Vivian's husband Mo offers Johnny some cash in hand for 'extra dance lessons' for his wife, because he will be busy playing cards all night. It took me even longer to understand that Johnny's decision to reject the offer of cash (and therefore reject Vivian herself) from Mo Pressman, in front of her, motivates her to report him to his boss for stealing the purses and wallets that have been going missing around the resort. This then leads to Baby having to expose their affair by providing his alibi, while accusing the old couple, the Schumachers (who are found to be the real thieves). 'I know he didn't take them,' she says falteringly, her eyes flicking briefly to her shocked father, 'I know he was in his room all night. And the reason I know . . . is because I was with him.' Wow – what a moment! Your heart could beat right out of your chest. She has just told everyone she is shagging the arse off her dancing instructor, right there, over breakfast.

There's a lot to learn from this film when you are 11 years old. The mysterious and complicated world of adults was slowly coming into focus for me, but a lot still went over my head. There are layers I missed the first time I watched *Dirty Dancing* that would later reveal themselves with repeat viewings (even to this day, Vivian Pressman is now a pretty vivid character for me, rather than a slightly tragic side-show). I remember around this period (the early 1990s) hearing the phrase, 'Hell hath no fury like a woman scorned', for example, and gaining some insight into its meaning because of Vivian's actions. To make herself feel better after Johnny's rejection, she goes straight to nasty Robbie Gould, the waiter, and is discovered on top of him by Lisa, Baby's sister, who arrives ready to let him pop her cherry. And all the while, a stone's throw away in another cabin, Johnny and Baby are having another world-beating shag. It's a busy night.

The moment where, in the harsh early morning light, a grim-faced Vivian, free of make-up, exits Robbie's cabin, and, as she tucks her tights into her evening bag, looks up to see Baby and Johnny, the image of wholesome sexuality, kissing each other goodbye after a night of love and tenderness, has got to be one of the bleakest images in romantic cinema. In fact, it has saved me from some seriously ill-advised, on-the-rebound-style hook ups over the years – I just picture myself as Vivian at dawn, still in her party dress, no tights, wondering who's using who, and it's enough to make me order a cab home. Thank you, Viv.

So now, let's deal with Neil. Poor Neil Kellerman represents all those men who inexplicably believe themselves to be catnip to women everywhere, when in fact they really couldn't be less sexually appealing. Even I, aged 11, understood that this man is not the one you want, even though he is intent on telling you that he is all you could ever dream of. He is the absolute antithesis of Johnny, and a sexual wasteland. A date with him would leave you about as moist as a beech-nut husk stranded in the midday sun. Mere mention of the line, 'I love to watch your hair blowing in the breeze', to any woman familiar with the film and therefore the scene where Neil invites Baby to come for an evening walk, will result in an instant and uncontrollable physical reaction of pure cringing disgust. Try it – honestly, you'll be amazed at the power those ten words can have. In fact, you don't even have to have seen the film.

Crucially, Neil can't dance. And this, to writer and retired dancer Eleanor Bergstein, essentially consigns any man to the sexual slag heap. For Bergstein, dancing is the greatest indicator of sexual prowess and compatibility. That's why it's called *Dirty Dancing*. Even more criminal than not being able to dance is not being able to dance while believing you can, a flaw Neil exhibits when he walks into the studio to talk to Johnny before the big end-of-season show. Baby tells him that she's just there to have some 'extra dance lessons'. We see Neil raise his hands, and gyrate a little, and utter the words, 'I can teach you, kid,' which will induce a vomit response in anyone who now firmly understands that dancing = sex. No, Neil, you can't. No, no, no.

But who am I to judge? Even though I knew every inch of what they were up to, how sex was and wasn't meant to be done, who to do it with – ideally – and when, what you should and shouldn't need to wear to get it, there was nothing much happening with me in that department in real life. It was, shall we politely say with a cough, 'theoretical'. That is, until I went to my first hip hop club in London, far from home, far from church, with a group of new and exciting friends I had met at a drama club.

I had always liked hip hop, rap, R'n'B – I can't say that I was particularly knowledgeable about them, or that my tastes within the genre were sophisticated, but they were unusual for the time and place I grew up. I went to a comprehensive school in Hertfordshire. It was mixed socially, but predominantly white. Most people were into guitar music and pop. I found bands such as Radiohead and Nirvana made me semi-suicidal, and instead hoovered up the likes of Arrested Development, The Fugees and Blackstreet, which were the bands in those genres that made it to the Top 40 in the 1990s. So although my tastes were uncommon in my little part of the Home Counties, I was still well within the parameters of what was available to buy from the music section of Woolworth's in town. There was nothing especially cool or underground about me – I just liked what I liked.

Dancing to Nirvana in a nightclub is very, very different to dancing to Blackstreet. Very. Different. The first time I went to a club playing this sort of music I was 17 years old, and – thanks to *Dirty Dancing* – I thought, 'Yes, this is it – this is what I want. I know how to do this.' And I dived in.

And it was here that I had my second ever snog, and let me say it was very, very different to the first one. Very. Different. It had started with dancing, some very, very dirty dancing, which resulted in a stern word from a friend as she pulled me away, looked me beadily in the eye, and told this naïve, 'watermelon carrying' suburban bumpkin that the 'only rule in the club tonight is you leave with who you came in with, OK?' I nodded dumbly, not quite understanding – of course I would leave with her, I didn't have anywhere else to stay. . . woaahhhhh, I see, I get it. She thought I might leave the club with this man I was dancing with, and stay at his house and have sex with him, and fuckinghellimonly17andimmeantobeachristianbutgodknowsidontfeelverychristiantonightandohgodimdancingwiththismanagainanditsjust.so.sexy.

Then he snogged me. And this man snogged me good and proper. There had been some fairly full-on dancing going until this point, but now some serious shit was happening. We weren't even dancing anymore, I was somehow just sitting on his lap at the side of the room, snogging his face off. He even put his finger in my mouth as we snogged, and somehow made it work. I have tried to recreate it since with other men, but generally it's an awful idea. Don't try it. I think you have to be drunk and recently dancing to Ginuwine's 'Pony' to pull it off.

This was a mini-epiphany for me. Actual sex wouldn't happen for another three years, and actual good sex a little time after that. But this was as close as I could imagine getting as a frigid, evangelical Christian virgin who didn't believe in sex before marriage. Was this my Johnny Castle, at last? I can't remember the man's name. I think he muttered something about being a 'driver' and that he would 'take care of me'. I'm not going to suggest that this was a marriage proposal, but it certainly felt romantic. He was a nice man. And a truly incredible kisser. He was quite a lot older than me. I don't remember any sense of feeling pressured by him to go somewhere else, so perhaps I was lucky, or unlucky. We could be happily married now – him doing his 'driving' to support us, and me at home with nine kids, still totally captivated by his ability to make putting a finger in your mouth while kissing an enjoyable experience. Who's to say what could have happened? Either way, I left the club with my friend, who practically body-checked me out the door, and as the hot sweat cooled onto my body in the night-time air, I felt heated from the inside. I felt like Baby. I felt like a woman.

You can do a lot worse than use *Dirty Dancing* as your guide through the sexual shenanigans of early youth. Baby is not a silent, smiling, swishy-haired princess. She is outspoken, noisy and casual in her appearance. She finds a man in Johnny who respects all of that, likes it, loves it, even. He only wants to lift her higher. Literally and figuratively. This film says, 'Find a man like Johnny, and go get him. Don't change yourself, change the world. Change the man if necessary. But remember: you're pretty in your own way. You don't have to change a thing.' It's a decent message for a teenage girl, better than 'drink fruit-flavoured laxatives to be thin', or 'shade your nose away with this beige pen', or 'take more clothes off to be noticed'. It's sexy, but it's equal. Everyone's at it, for good and bad reasons. It's messy.

But that's life, and that's sex. You can't make it tidy, so you might as well enjoy it.

3
De Todo Un Poco

7.30pm, 13 March 2010.

The show is *Let's Dance for Sport Relief*, a charity that raises money for African and UK aid projects, and it's going out live to an audience of 8 million people.

I am stood on the world's shiniest floor, behind two large sliding black doors, beyond which are nine TV cameras, a live studio audience, a panel of judges, presenters Mel and Sue and my new fiancé.

Thirty seconds to performance.

I am wearing a black leotard, a glove made of shards of mirrored glass, three pairs of tights, a pair of strappy heels and a lot of gold body make-up.

Twenty seconds to performance.

I can hear Mel and Sue begin my introduction. Standing

in front of me are two professional dancers, wearing the same leotard as me, minus the glove, each with about 70 per cent less thigh than I have.

Ten seconds to performance.

I can hear the end of the video clips package. I am shaking uncontrollably. It's fear, yes, but also adrenaline. More adrenaline than I have ever felt running through my body in my entire life. I wonder if this much adrenaline is actually safe. I wonder if I might need a paramedic.

Five seconds to performance.

They are saying my name. The music starts. The doors start to slide back. And I can see only bright lights as we move forward in line. I'm supposed to be strutting sassily, but I can barely walk because I'm shaking so much. Am I dying? Possibly. But it's too late to stop now. Beyoncé's 'Single Ladies' starts playing and the rest is noise. Blur and noise.

Oh god. I still feel sick now, and I'm only writing it down.

At the time of writing, the YouTube video of me performing the 'Single Ladies' dance has nearly 40 million hits. Every year, a TV company in Japan enquires about my availability to perform on Japanese national TV, competing against their leading Beyoncé impersonator. Every year, I say yes, and then ask for a fee so ludicrous that I never hear from them again. Until the following year, when a fresh enquiry is made. They truly believe that doing the 'Single Ladies' dance is my main occupation. They think I am the UK's leading Beyoncé impersonator, and therefore a worthy opponent for their own home-grown Queen B. And with YouTube numbers like that, who can blame them? They do not know that between then and now I have lived through a somewhat gritty labour, and giving birth to a baby with an unusually large head has left me rather less able to slut drop suddenly or convincingly.

The 'Single Ladies' dance is still usually the first thing anyone says about me on introductions to panel shows, live events, and other appearances on TV, radio and the stage. It's in my official CV. People put the song on at weddings, meaning I am forced to hide until it's over, otherwise all the other guests form a circle around me and clap until I drunkenly agree to attempt as much of it as I can remember. I performed a version of the dance on my 2010 tour, dressed in full military gear as a butch soldier character I invented called Captain Rosie, closing the first half of the show to a standing ovation more often than not. Years after the event, a man booked me for a gig on the basis that I would perform 'Single Ladies', but he didn't tell me that in advance, and even though I explicitly said I would be doing normal stand-up, he didn't listen and was so furious that my act was 'Single Ladies'-less, he didn't want to pay me.

In terms of reach and endurability, nothing else I have ever done comes close. I had three series of an award-winning sketch show, I was in the very episode of *Peep Show* which was voted the most popular ever, I've written a novel – A WHOLE NOVEL, FOR PITY'S SAKE – I've met Prince Philip *and* Dame Emma Thompson. I've met THE POPE. And yet all these things might as well not exist, when set alongside three minutes of 'Single Ladies'-based exertion in 2010.

And I don't even mind. My greatest triumph was

expressed through the medium of dance, and I sort of love that. And it was a really fucking difficult dance at that. I'm not going to lie – it nearly killed me. We had five days of rehearsal: that was the rule. Everyone in the competition was only allowed five days of rehearsal, no matter what dance they were doing. Which is both fair and not fair at the same time.

I turned up to the rehearsal room on the morning of day one feeling nervous, but certain that the choreographer and two professional dancers would have the whole routine worked out, and they would simply teach it to me. It would be tough – I wasn't really fit enough to do it justice. But it was a comedy show, and so long as I learned the basic steps and messed about a bit in the middle, we would be fine. We had loads of time . . .

I walked in to see three people in tracksuits crowded round a laptop, watching a YouTube video with the kind of intense concentration I imagine is normally reserved for moon landings. I wandered over and introduced myself. They looked up and smiled, and at that point I clocked that they were in fact watching the official video of Beyoncé's 'Single Ladies'. On YouTube. Like anyone can. 'Oh hi,' said the choreographer. 'We were just trying to figure out the dance. . . it's incredibly complicated, isn't it?'

Oh shit.

Yes, it is incredibly complicated. I knew this because I had also been watching the official video on YouTube at home, and had, until this point, been relieved that someone else would have already figured it out and would simply teach it to me.

'Come and have a look and see if you can work out this step here,' he said.

'Which step?' I said.

'The first one.'

Shit, shit, shit.

We were already 20 minutes into day one – Monday. I would dance this for the first and possibly the last time ON SATURDAY. I thought about simply running away. Literally, just running out of the room and not coming back. There was no way I could learn this dance in five days if my teachers didn't know it either. But instead, I laughed jauntily to cover my panic (a frequent tactic of mine) and bent over the laptop to have a look.

Well, we did it, somehow. The dancers – Steph and Stefanie – were amazing. We practised for hours and hours. My fiancé had to rub my legs every night, and I was so sore I could only go up or downstairs sideways, like a giant crab. But we did it. And now almost 40 million people have watched it. It's my most popular piece of work by about 39.99999 million hits. Those three minutes of film may outlast every other thing I ever do. It might even outlast me. So I am a dancer. I must be. There's simply no other explanation. I am the Florence Foster Jenkins of the dance world – they can say I didn't dance well, but they can't say I didn't dance.

So, with my credentials now beyond doubt, let's turn to *Dirty Dancing*. Written by a former dancer, it was always going to be a love letter to the form. It is as if Eleanor Bergstein really wanted to write about what's it like to be a professional hoofer, and somehow created a record-breaking romantic drama by accident. And as a girl she had experienced the world she created, the very world of *Dirty Dancing*, as her parents took her to a resort in the Catskills and played golf while she danced with the professional staff. She later referred to herself as a 'teenage Mambo queen'.

The stories each of the main characters tell of how they got into dance themselves, specifically Johnny and Penny, show how dance somehow scooped them up as lost kids and rescued them. 'My mother kicked me out when I was 16,' says Penny to the wide-eyed Baby, 'I've been dancing ever since. It was all I ever wanted to do anyway.' Bergstein wants to show that dancing can save you, and so the actual moves needed to be spectacular.

The film was choreographed by Kenny Ortega, who had trained with Gene Kelly, but this was his first big gig. He made a stellar career off the back of the film, including choreographing and directing the smash-hit *High School Musical* franchise. If you would like to get a sense of Ortega's personal style, please enjoy the behind the scenes footage of him taking dance rehearsals for *High School Musical* on the DVD extras, which clearly shows him teaching his choreography to the cast while holding a small dog in his arms throughout. That's Hollywood.

But the man knew what he was doing, and though 'iconic' is an overused word these days, it is appropriate for the sequences he created in *Dirty Dancing*. There's wit and verve, but also romance, sex, beauty, tension and drama, all conveyed through dance. Now, I'm no Shirley Ballas (no, really, I'm not . . .) so I'm not going to attempt an ill-advised technical analysis of the Latin Dance choreography on offer, but I know amazing, spine-tingling moves when I see them.

The first time we see Johnny and his professional partner Penny do what they do best is when they arrive at the evening function at Kellerman's, where other guests are dancing to a live band. In they come, and suddenly the world crackles. Penny in her sparkling pink dress, Johnny in his black DJ and very well-fitting high-waisted black trousers. There's a pause in the music. A new song begins, and BAM, they start dancing. I swear to god, I felt thrills running up and down my body like never before. There were goosebumps the size of limpets on my arms. I could only gurgle. I felt lit from the inside. I thought, 'I want to do THAT.'

The moment I remember most is when Penny puts her leg on Johnny's shoulder during this very first dance sequence. He then drags her along the floor in a kind of diagonal splits move, her other foot on the ground behind her. My eyes popped so far out of my head you could've hung your coat on them. Once I had my prize safely committed to video tape, I re-wound and re-wound this scene. I tried to re-enact it with my little sister, but found that it doesn't work if you are taller than your partner – you just end up awkwardly walking over them.

All the dancing feels spontaneous throughout, like it's emanating from them and they can't help it. This is partly because the steps themselves had a very spontaneous and 'lived' provenance. In an interview Kenny Ortega gave to American broadcaster National Public Radio, he said, '[it was] street salsa, Colombian-style salsa, Cuban rhythm step, R&B

and street soul – we were drawing from a number of different places to ultimately arrive at what *Dirty Dancing* became.' These dances came from professionals enjoying themselves together, creating new steps in their own time and at parties. The joy you see overflowing from them as they dance is real – it was based on Bergstein's own experiences of dirty dancing in basements in Brooklyn during the 1960s.

Thousands of miles away, over on the West Coast in California, Ortega had also been trying new steps with his own friends. The two of them came together at the right time, with the right moves, and created a phenomenon. When we see Johnny eagerly try to explain a 'new step he's been working on' to Neil Kellerman, who remains unimpressed and merely threatens to fire him, it comes from lived experience. Dancers like Johnny Castle, known to both Bergstein and Ortega, would have been working on their own new fusion steps all the time. This creativity is what inspired all the choreography.

Ortega was thorough too, understanding that for the evolution of Baby's dance ability to work over the course of the narrative, he needed to pay attention to the details. Bergstein recalls in the same interview: 'He went over everything with me. You know, "Did Baby dance on her father's feet when she was a little girl?" We went over all the basic subtext of how I wanted everybody to move in it because he wanted to know everything.'

The love story is also intimately bound up with the dance story for Bergstein; she has said that the moment Johnny falls in love with Baby is when she is unable to do the lift when they perform the show dance at the Sheldrake

Hotel, and instead of freezing and panicking, she does a little improvised shimmy with her hands. A move many of us have adopted in moments of awkwardness, only to find that the people we are with aren't familiar enough with *Dirty Dancing* to know what we're doing. So you end up looking like you're just doing some odd and inappropriate hand dancing simply because you've forgotten the name of a colleague who has recently died (Look, I barely knew him).

Since seeing *Dirty Dancing* for the first time, I have fantasised about being taught to dance properly by a partner – who hasn't?! It doesn't have to lead to sex. I just love dancing. I love the controlled intimacy of it, the freedom within boundaries, and the way you can explore your feelings without having to say a word. So I had to have a little sit down on the stairs a few years ago when I got a call from my agent: 'I've just had *Strictly* on the phone. Would you like to do the Christmas special?'

'YES.'

It was short notice – someone had dropped out. My partner would be Anton Du Beke, and we would perform the Viennese waltz. Not the sexiest of scenarios, but a blessing in many ways – it had been many years since I had last (successfully) done the splits, and I didn't fancy Anton's chances of lifting me over his head. So even though it would not be my hot and steamy Latin dream come true, it was likely that something rather more dignified and stately, such as the waltz, would be the best option for maintaining some level of self-respect.

This was it – it was really happening. I would have to learn a dance at short notice in order to cover for someone who had a personal emergency. Wait, what? LIKE BABY, YOU SAY? Why yes, yes – now you mention it . . . JUST LIKE BABY.

My life is mostly words, words, words. I write words, read words, learn words, speak words. That is 98 per cent of my job. Occasionally, I get to sing words, but not often. My head is so full of words all the time, I have to write some of them down else I'd go completely insane. But oh, sometimes it's just nice to forget them all, and have some other language take over. Thanks to *Dirty Dancing*, the dream of dancing still has tentacles, wrapped somewhere around my soul. So, whenever an opportunity arises, I grab at it.

Christmas *Strictly* 2012 was just such an opportunity, and I was so into it, it was ridiculous. I was in heaven from the moment we started rehearsing. You have to give in to it, to surrender totally – the schedule is huge, and you are only a cog in it. They tell you when a car is coming to collect you and when it will take you home. You are then theirs for the day. You get driven around to costume fittings, and make-up tests, and spray tanning sessions – in fact, portable tanning booths are set up in dedicated dressing rooms and you are allowed, no, positively *encouraged* to use them. Any moment where nothing much is happening, and the action is elsewhere, you can pop in for a tan top-up. This is why everyone with paler skin tones on *Strictly* is such a crazy colour – you can get sprayed any time you're bored, and you do. You become the colour of an oak wardrobe because you never see another person outside of the *Strictly* bubble – you literally forget what colour you normally are: you lose your perspective, but it doesn't matter. And somewhere, somehow, in the midst of it all, you learn a dance.

The night of the recording came. I did my dance. It wasn't too nerve-racking as it wasn't live. And Anton was there beside me, muttering the moves into my ear as we sped round and round. There were no lifts to contend with, and I knew the routine backwards as we had rehearsed a lot – I think possibly more than he was used to, given some of his previous partners. I wanted to do it well, I wanted to do it right. Most of all, I wanted that weightless, wordless sensation that comes when you hit the right steps in the right order, and the dancing just takes over. I wasn't going to win – I wasn't trying to. I wasn't as good as some of the others that night. I forgot about everything when the music started and my arms raised and circled and we began. For three minutes, I forgot everything else in the world. That's what dancing is for. That's what dancing can do.

The pro-dancers on the show are super-human beacons of positivity, constantly telling everyone how great they look, how wonderful the dancing is, so that you feel you never want to leave. I have no doubt that there are private rows, stresses and breakdowns, but something about the show works its magic, and at the appointed time each week you have to drop everything and just dance. Your divorce, your clicky knee, your scary letter from your accountant will all have to wait.

It's dancing time, and nothing else matters. This is why you see contestants cry on the main show and say they don't ever want it to stop. They mean it. The pale world that awaits them on expulsion seems chilly and flat by comparison. *Strictly* is show-biz in its purest form. It is TV Kellerman's.

But the job I had that got me closest to vicariously experiencing the actual *Dirty Dancing* life took place in hot and steamy southern Italy in 2013. It was a musical film called *Walking on Sunshine*, with about 40 professional dancers to make us in the main cast look better than we were. We had a top-level choreographer who worked her arse off on some truly incredible routines. The actors and dancers, and crew, pushed ourselves to our limits for the cameras every day, and every night there would effectively be a huge party as the limitless energy of these super-fit athletes of the art world felt they hadn't done enough dancing for the day, and so went out for a full night of dance on their own time. Reader, I couldn't keep up. But I tried, oh god, I tried, because this was the real deal.

I also learnt about how hard it is to be a professional dancer, and how badly treated they are in many professional jobs. They have no agents, they have no union. They're tough. When two dancers arrived to find they had no accommodation booked for the night, what did they do? Arranged to sleep on the floor of other people's hotel rooms and went out dancing for the night. They'd solve the problem in the morning. This is what I love about dancing – it's immediate. You hear some music that catches you and your body reacts before your mind. You just start moving.

And oh my god, those dancers were unbelievably good. All of them. They let us come along for the ride, and I didn't even have to carry a watermelon. They were unstoppable, and the *Dirty Dancing* was quite . . . remarkable. They were all commercial dancers, which meant they did pop videos mostly – they were incredibly sexy and totally uninhibited. They seemed to live in the moment; literally any time some music came on in any scenario, under any circumstances, they would all start dancing. And nobody minds. At times, it started to resemble an orgy where only the smallest pieces of cloth prevented actual penetration.

Because feeling confident in your body and what it can do is sexy – you can't help it, when you feel good about your body, good enough to spontaneously move it to music, your sex appeal goes up by about 400 per cent. And this is the crucial element of Baby's story in *Dirty Dancing* – getting comfortable with her body. In the dance at the Sheldrake, she looks embarrassed throughout, and there's nothing powerful, exciting, or sexy about it. But later, in Johnny's cabin, they start to move together properly, and her confidence in what her body can now do takes over. You could argue that the control she now feels over her physical being means she is ready for the next step. She is not embarrassed or ashamed, it just happens.

And the equality and trust in dancing with someone else plays an important part – there's a message in *Dirty Dancing* that is clear: if you trust someone enough to dance with them, with all your being, to even let them lift you high in the air, you can trust them with anything. The dancers in the story are fundamentally good people, honest people, because there's an honesty in what they do for a living – your body can't lie, it can only express what's deep within. This is why in Eleanor Bergstein's world, the dishonest people are the ones who can't dance – Neil, Lisa, Robbie – they can't move well because they are not properly connected to themselves. It's not a scientifically proven theory – I wouldn't like to see it peer reviewed by leading biologists in the *New Scientist*, but perhaps a representative group of my *Dirty Dancing*-loving peers would back me up in a Johnny Castle fan-fic site, and that's good enough for me.

The noble suffering in dancing, and being a dancer is also reflected in the film, in fiction and reality. During the filming of the famous final dance, including 'the lift', Patrick Swayze was dealing with a severe knee injury, and the whole thing was agony. God knows how many times they had to perform it for the cameras – I know when I was making the film in Italy, we did each dance routine around 20 times a day, sometimes in 44-degree heat. You finish one take, then you walk back to your opening position to the ever optimistic cry of, 'Just one more, please, straight away again!' and do it 'once more' as if it's the first time. I felt uncomfortable a lot (mostly because many of my costumes were 90 per cent polyester, including my wig and shoes, which meant I was essentially laminated from head to foot), but after a cold shower, I was always buzzing to do it all again.

Hotel owner Max Kellerman bemoans his falling profits, as he says his Catskills resort is going out of fashion. 'Kids these days want trips to Europe,' he says, not a load of fuddy-duddy dance lessons from a by-gone age. In a sweetly hopeful line in the final scene, he suddenly sees a bright future for his hotel, if he can bring some teachable form of this Latin hybrid going on all around him to the young people of America, and revive his fortunes.

It was never going to happen, and the Catskills are not what they once were in their 1960s heyday. But *Dirty Dancing* did get teenagers like me revved up about the notion of dancing with a partner, rather than standing in long lines along a rigid biological sex-based divide at the school disco and dancing in front of each other. It was followed in later years by the unexpected and wildly popular Australian film, *Strictly Ballroom*, which of course gave our dear BBC the idea of reviving its ancient *Come Dancing* formula by merely sticking the word 'Strictly' on the front of it. Suddenly it was modern and a bit ironic. And now it's the highest rated BBC entertainment show on TV by miles.

The best thing about dancing with a partner is the trust, and this is something I have learned from watching dance films and working with professional dancers. Trust is the central theme of *Dirty Dancing* too, with its storylines dealing with theft, lying and integrity. A dance partnership has to be an equal relationship or it doesn't work. Observing the professional dancers I have worked with, it is clear that they all respect one another. Whether other people in other parts of the entertainment industry respect them is another matter, but they know better than to treat one another badly. If you are physically throwing yourself around, relying on someone to catch you, lift you, support you, or stay in exact time with you, there must be a mutual respect or it doesn't work.

Dirty Dancing models this perfectly for any young person – and not just girls, even though it is Baby's story. We see her grow in confidence – the outfits change for a start, and I remember wondering, 'WHERE DID ALL THIS PROFESSIONAL DANCER KIT APPEAR FROM THEN, EH??' I concluded she had either a) borrowed it from Penny, or b) that there was some sort of dancewear shop on site. But the point is, Baby wants to show the sweat and muscle she is making. At one point, she even appears to have a small six-pack – it's about her strength as well as her sexuality.

One of the reasons Baby and Johnny form an instant connection is that they have straight-talking personalities. And I've found there's very little bullshit with dancers in general, or at least the ones I have worked with. They are often very intuitive and sensitive, reading people well with excellent instincts and an ability to read body language – it stands to reason, given that they must be so attuned to their physicality. It's hard to lie to a dancer. I have always liked their company too, as they just say it like it is and you don't constantly feel that you are trying to de-code something. Truths are offered, often with a shrug, and then a suggestion of where we could go that plays great music.

Eleanor Bergstein wanted to write a film about dancers, and the importance of dance, as if it has a morality of its own. Johnny is the most morally upright character in the film and I think that was the intention. Dancers are good people – dance makes you a better person.

After all, dance is all about trust, hard work, taking risks, becoming connected with your body, enjoying yourself, and just generally letting go.

You have to be prepared to look ridiculous, or out of control. And once you give in, it's such a relief. And a release. A good dance can be the best medicine, equal only to a good laugh in terms of health benefits. A friend of mine who is an actress of immense stature, known for her thoughtful, dignified and intelligent performances, has taken to giving parties in the last few years where she makes sure the live band plays at such a high volume that conversation is practically impossible. She doesn't want to talk, and she doesn't want anyone else to feel they have to either. The music is fantastic. She dances all night, pausing only every so often to dash around the room being a good host, introducing people to each other in a flash of movement before heading back to the dance floor. You have no choice but to dance in the end. People who would usually never dance, who want to find a quiet corner for a chat, end up sweaty and gyrating with everyone else, because there simply are no quiet corners. You go home happy and with your ears ringing like they haven't in years. And everyone, absolutely everyone, says it's the best party they have been to in a long time. No conversation; only dancing. What a gift. What therapy.

I love it. I love dancing. But it's not my job, and it never could be. It occasionally forms part of my job, and I love those times. But obviously, I'm not good enough to be a professional, nowhere near, and I never could have been. But thanks to *Dirty Dancing*, it is in me now and I can throw off my self-consciousness and get to that higher plane where the moves are all that matter. And it's really not important if you're not the greatest dancer either – anyone having a wonderful time, enjoying the music, enjoying the feeling of unspoken expression, will always be winning. Dancing is for everyone.

If in doubt, dance. That's a good rule for life.

4
Big Girls Don't Cry

*O*ne of the great joys of repeat viewings of *Dirty Dancing* is how it grows with you. I never thought, when I first saw it aged 11, that I would be getting parenting tips from it, but here we are, 30 years later, and I'm tearfully accepting that sometimes you have to apologise to your children for getting something wrong, though you'd probably rather drink a pint of vinegar. Even the most perfect parents are not exempt from learning this lesson the hard way, as Eleanor Bergstein shows through her striking and moving portrayal of the relationship between Baby and her father.

Dr Jake Houseman is almost too good to be true. A respected physician, a good husband, a loving father to two girls, and certainly a man who deserves a holiday after working so hard for years, looking after others. He has even treated hotel proprietor Max Kellerman, who claims he saved his life: 'Ladies, if it wasn't for your father, I'd be standing here dead,' he tells the Houseman women when they arrive.

What Dr Jake Houseman is looking for is three restful weeks in the Catskills at a luxury resort with his beautiful family. He's probably paid an awful lot of money for this privilege. He thinks he's going to head home feeling refreshed and revived. His lovely elder daughter Lisa is not going to be heading any NASA missions any time soon, but it doesn't matter – she wants to get married, settle down and have kids. A traditional woman. And as for his younger daughter Baby, well, he couldn't be more proud – she's headstrong and intelligent, and though he worries for her a little because he knows the world is not always a good place, he feels certain that he will always be able to protect her from harm, because he's strong and decent, and has brought her up right. He's a liberal man – he's seen things, but he believes in progress. With his glamorous and elegant wife Marge at his side, they can enter a new phase in their lives where perhaps he can take things a little easier now. Perhaps his work is done.

Well.

He didn't bank on Johnny Castle and the sheer transformative power of dance. He also didn't bank on his own daughter, Baby, being the one to break away from his sphere of influence so decidedly that he has to re-evaluate everything he thought he knew.

Jake Houseman expects Baby to marry an educated man, perhaps a man who he fondly thinks will, 'remind her of her old dad'. Perhaps a lot of men with daughters have this private hope. And it's not without merit, after all, in the opening voiceover Baby herself says, 'I thought I'd never find a guy as great as my dad.' This sentiment, curiously American in flavour, has always struck me as a bit weird. You're going to compare every guy you find attractive to your father, until you find one just like him? OK. Not me. But it certainly throws down an emotional gauntlet – is any man equal to the task ahead? What will it take to pull Baby from the trusted embrace of her father? Someone pretty special, no doubt . . .

We know what Jake expects of his daughter, because Baby later speaks his words back to him in the heartbreaking autumnal scene which takes place in an empty lakeside gazebo (note the props assistant throwing handfuls of dried brown leaves over the camera lens as it zooms in on Jerry Orbach looking pensive). It is the end of summer, and the end of something else too. Baby says, 'You wanted me to change the world but you meant by becoming a lawyer or an economist and marrying someone from Harvard.' Now, there's nothing wrong with this in itself, but clearly, at this point, Baby disagrees that it's her only acceptable or viable path in life. 'You said I let you down. But you let me down too, Daddy.' And he looks away, unable to hold in his tears.

Any parent whose grown-up child stands in front of them and says 'You let me down', is going to feel that sharply. And Baby is the kind of character who demands to be taken seriously, in spite of her nickname. She has a way with words. She is persuasive. She would, ironically, make a great lawyer. Throughout *Dirty Dancing*, she gets people to do and say things they could never have dreamed of doing and saying, while also doing and saying previously unimaginable things herself. Johnny shouts at her in loving frustration, 'You look at the world and see how it should be; if someone's lost, you find them, if something's broken, you fix it – what you did for me, standing up for me like that, I've never had anyone do anything like that for me before.' And you believe him. She is quite a remarkable young woman.

But to her father, she has always been his Baby and, as sister Lisa points out, his favourite. Until the trouble with Penny is uncovered, that is, and it all comes apart. 'He listens when I talk now,' Lisa says with bitter triumph after Baby's perceived fall from grace, 'and you hate that.'

Baby's mother, Marge Houseman, on the other hand, is a slight presence throughout the whole film, until the very last moment where she tells her husband to sit down as he rises in indignation at Johnny reappearing to lead his daughter towards the stage – that 'Sit down, Jake' has some power to it, and you realise perhaps she has been more awake to what's going on than she seems. It's the only moment she asserts anything and it's all the more striking for it. The rest of her chat is mostly inane, or apparently oblivious. When her husband comes back in the middle of the night after dealing with the aftermath of Penny's botched abortion, she sleepily murmurs, 'Is everything alright?' and then goes straight back to sleep when she's told to. If that were me, I would be bolt upright, lights on, demanding to know EXACTLY what had been going on.

And when Marge witnesses the conversation on the golf course between Baby and her father, about randomly lending her $250 in cash by the end of the day, in the middle of what is essentially a fully-paid up trip to an all-inclusive resort in a mountain forest, she merely looks on smiling blankly. If that were me, I would be striding over with my hands on my hips, demanding to know what the money was for, and why the urgency? Is there not enough chicken and pineapple on the buffet? Have they run out of orange juice? Does she need *extra dance lessons?* DO YOU TAKE ME FOR A FOOL, CHILD? Now, What. Is. Going. On . . .? But maybe that's just me. I am a pain in the arse, as my children will no doubt confirm in due course.

So, the focus is really on Baby's relationship with her father and how that is threatened and ultimately superseded by her relationship with Johnny. Mother is a little bit off the reservation . . . maybe a Valium or two? Who are we to judge? She has clearly brought up two lovely, and very different girls. I'll leave Marge alone now – you can't have every character in a film front and centre or it gets too crowded. One of *Dirty Dancing*'s strengths is its focus – it knows what it wants to say.

Eleanor Bergstein is clearly interested in the way a girl leaves the protection of her father and becomes a woman in her own right, rather than examining mother/daughter relationships in detail. There are dozens of rite-of-passage films about boys learning to become men, and perhaps having to deal with a more realistic view of their own fathers as a result – everything from *Big* to *The Karate Kid* to *Star Wars*, to pick just three. But there are very few about girls and fathers, or father-figures – perhaps we can count *Labyrinth*, but I am struggling to think of more.

I have always felt deeply uncomfortable around men who say, even as a joke, that any prospective boyfriend their daughter may desire will 'have to get past me first'. It's become a trope, and a cliché now. And many people still seem to think it's a positive emotion, showing how protective a good man is over the honour of his precious little girl. But it has always smacked of ownership to me, and some outdated insistence on a girl's virginity at marriage. Why should any father get to intimidate a man his daughter, in her good judgement, has chosen for herself? Like the father of the bride tradition of giving away his daughter to the groom, it implies that the woman is a possession, albeit a precious and well-cared-for one.

Dirty Dancing plays with this, but backs away from anything too confrontational. It is more that it is in the air – it's the subtext. But given that Baby manages to have a full-blown affair that lasts at least a week, right under her parents' noses, suggests they are not so controlling. Lisa too is getting it on with Robbie the waiter. It makes you wonder what Jake and Marge Houseman think is going on when their daughters' shared bedroom in the family cabin is empty night after night. Perhaps they are too busy getting busy themselves – all that golf and fresh air, and the dancing lessons, of course – perhaps there is a sock on the door handle of Pater and Mater Houseman's room for the bulk of the holiday? And after each marital encounter, they share one of Marge's Valiums and tuck down for the night? Who knows? But until the moment Baby shakes her father awake and silently hands him his doctor's bag to go to Penny's aid, they seem blissfully ignorant of anything that has been going on.

When you have teenagers, you never really know what's going on. You can do the best you can to be involved enough to have a pretty good idea, but ultimately, you don't know. Teenagers can be highly secretive, while appearing to be completely open and honest. I know this because I've been one, and also raised one. Friends of mine have asked in terrified anticipation of their own children's approaching teenage years, 'How do you cope with it?' And I say, 'I still have no idea. Just accept that they're going to lie to you, no matter how cool and progressive you are.'

I always kept this in the back of my mind as a parent to a teenager – if we were getting on well, and all seemed transparent and open, I would feel happy, but not too smug, because you just never really know. I've had so many parents of 15/16-year-olds look me in the eye and say, 'He just genuinely doesn't seem interested in drink or drugs – honestly, we chat about it all the time so I think I'd know. I like to believe it's because we gave him bits of wine on holiday in France when he was a kid, you know, like the French do. I think it stopped booze being a big deal.' And they happily sip their glass of crisp Chablis, while you know almost for certain that their darling child is dealing weed at school and lining up Jägerbombs for breakfast.

It is amazing how blissfully unaware you can be of what's really going on. Teenagers do secret squirrel like nothing else on earth. In her book on growing up in suburbia, *Another Planet*, singer Tracey Thorn writes brilliantly on the teenage need to lie to parents, regardless of how successful and empathetic the parenting has been: 'Teenagers NEED to lie. It doesn't mean that parenting has failed. It's part of the process of breaking away, and forging a separate identity.' Thank god.

And in fact, I always feel more worried for teenagers who say they tell their parents everything. But then I remember they're probably lying about that too, and I feel better.

So Baby has to lie to make this rite-of-passage story work. It's not the sex, it's the lie that kicks everything off. 'It's not illegal, is it?' says Jake on the golf course, as Baby holds out her hand. Baby swallows unconvincingly. 'No, Daddy,' she replies, and that is enough for him. He trusts her so completely he just hands her the money for something that is, in fact, completely illegal. I've had more rigorous interrogations over the loan of £20, with which I intended to buy a giant Michael J. Fox poster and pin it to my ceiling (word of advice – it's really hard to pin a two-metre-long poster to a bedroom ceiling on your own, and anyone observing you through your bedroom window as you try is going to have a really good laugh at your expense).

It's an interesting lie Baby chooses to tell. She does it to help Penny, who needs the money to pay for the termination for her pregnancy. Her motivation is purely to help another woman in need. So she's not choosing a sexual relationship with a man over the relationship with her father. She is not aware until after she hands over the money that she will need to step in as cover for Penny for the show dance at the Sheldrake. It is an act of female solidarity. No doubt she is intrigued by the backstage scene, and the fact that dancing with Johnny set her womb on fire means she would like an excuse to hang out with these people more, get in their good books, maybe gyrate with Johnny a couple more times. But really, she just wants to help – we have seen this from her choice of reading material (*The Plight of the Peasant* is the book in her hands in the first scene), and helping Billy (twice – the bags, and then the watermelon), and of course in her plans for the future. It's this desire to rescue someone, anyone, that moves us to the next stage of her journey.

I related to all of this, as I hoovered up viewing after viewing of *Dirty Dancing*. I was a headstrong, wilful teenager. I was bloody-minded, determined, stubborn and pushy. I lied frequently to my parents, although I wasn't doing anything particularly bad – I just didn't like the idea of anyone knowing what I was up to. My bedroom door was adorned with home-made 'Keep Out' posters, and my teenage diaries all had a front page telling any snoopers that although I couldn't stop them reading on, I hoped their conscience would prevent it. Yes, I was using psychological warfare, even at the age of 12. Not that I included anything interesting in my diaries. I always wrote entries with the kind of caution that one would usually employ if you were expecting them to one day be read out in court as evidence against you. So I was even lying to myself. Baby is a much, much nicer person than I am. I was always preoccupied with some trivial matter, like who got to sing a longer solo in the school concert, or whether I could get away with wiping the bathroom with a tea-towel rather than properly cleaning it.

But that sense of determination and drive was familiar to me – refusing to take no for an answer, saying I can do something even when I'm not sure I really can, pushing, pushing, pushing. Part of becoming a Christian at 13, which I did on my own without my family making me or anything (yup), was to satisfy this need for purpose. I always liked being part of a project, preferably with a big finale of some kind. Concerts, plays, prom committees, charitable activities such as sleeping rough for a night, or re-decorating a hostel for the homeless – something where there was a big reveal and you build up to it, go all out, enjoy the applause and praise, and then collapse. Until the next thing. This is my rhythm, and I'm going to say now, it's not very good for my health. But it's too late now – this is who I am.

When Baby decides to help, she goes for it. There is no hesitation, and no question that she will let anybody down. And endearingly, you see these same traits in her father. She wakes him up in the middle of the night and he simply follows her to the trouble, no questions asked. She is very much her father's daughter, which is why she is his favourite (you get the feeling that Marge and Lisa could discuss coral shoes, lipstick shades and honeymoon destinations for the entire three weeks, given half a chance). Presumably the kind of father–daughter discussions they have had led Baby to act with this level of confidence and assurance at the age of 17.

I was also lucky enough to grow up in a house where the discussion of ideas was encouraged, and I have tried to do the same as a parent. Of course, it can get uncomfortable, but is there anything more thrilling than being challenged by your own children? Well, that's what I like to tell myself after yet another ego-bruising encounter – better this way than silence and alienation. But then on the flip side, the memories of my teenage self, flinging my righteous ideals around as if nothing else in the world was so important, are still fresh and also make me cringe a little.

My problem was – who am I kidding? – my problem *is* that I always want more. I always want the next thing. I campaign as hard as I can for something, then I get it, and within ten minutes, I have identified something else I want, and I start the campaign for that. And so it goes on. It applies to everything – work, travel, food, drink, people – I don't want to keep still and I'm no good at counting my blessings and smelling the roses. I'll count my blessings, but then think, 'Wouldn't one more be nice? How can I get it?' I'll smell the roses and think, 'Well, that's the roses dealt with – I wonder what *those* flowers smell like?'

My point is that I was hard work as a teenager, and rows were inevitable. Many of the rows were caused by me wanting something that was either, a) madly expensive and therefore unaffordable, or b) almost impossible. Sometimes I would combine the two, and really dig in. One memorable year, during my Michael Jackson obsession (I repeat this was the early 1990s, and NOBODY KNEW), he announced tour dates to the UK. I had never seen Michael Jackson live at that point and I was so desperate to that it made my stomach hurt.

When I discovered that I wouldn't be able to go because the dates fell right in the middle weekend of our usual fortnight's camping holiday in Cornwall, I was devastated. My parents shook their heads sadly, and I guess they thought that would be that – game over. Well, it wasn't. I kept my onslaught of tears going for weeks. I cried so loudly in my bed every night that nobody could sleep. I took to bursting into tears at random, unexpected moments. The rest of the time I maintained a sullen silence, refusing to join in with anything. They would not budge. I shouted, I tore my hair, I begged, I pleaded. Still, no. The holiday was booked. It was paid for. You can't always get what you want. He would tour again one day. I thought I might die and not even care.

And then, a miracle occurred. Michael Jackson added two further dates to his London leg. And those two dates fell a week after we got back from holiday. I dashed home ready to impart the news, wondering what they would say, given my dreadful behaviour about it all.

When my dad returned from work that day, I was ready to burst, but he looked like he already had something to tell me. And he did. The moment those dates were added that morning, he had got on the phone to the booking line, re-dialling and re-dialling until he got through (ah, the past . . . it's a different country), and when at last he did, he had bought four tickets – for my parents, my little sister and me. I remember literally screaming for joy.

Ultimately, Michael Jackson was not someone you want for an idol, we know that now. But I will never forget the moment when I was told I was going, that it had been taken care of. My dad had sorted it out. Dads are supposed to sort things out, to some extent. That is what is expected of them. And it is Baby's natural and immediate instinct when things go wrong to go to her father.

The theme of broken families raises its head as Johnny sneers at Baby when she produces an envelope of cash to hand to Penny for her abortion, still uncertain of her character or motives for helping. 'Yeah, takes a real saint to ask Daddy,' he says, barely able to look at her, and swigs his beer in disgust. The dancers don't have daddies to run to – that is made clear. They have only themselves to rely on, and must watch on each summer as a new batch of spoilt, pampered children enjoy a luxury break with their parents, sealed in a bubble of privilege.

But Baby attempts to break out of the bubble, as she clearly craves something more gritty and exciting than she's experienced so far in her life. And you could argue that it is the solid foundation she has in her family and their financial security that gives her the confidence to act as she does. Those of us born and brought up in broadly safe, comfortable, middle-class homes are too often unaware how it feels to really be 'out there' on your own, with no back up and no one to bail you out. Baby's example (hang around the cool kids until you can make yourself useful) is the route into that world for girls like me. And by 'like me', I mean square. Square girls, who fancy themselves a bit intellectual, but run a mile when they encounter anything too gritty and have never really been in a situation where no one will help you. Yes, I had my share of not being able to get home from a party and having to sit on a war memorial until the buses started running again, but that's not exactly living dangerously. I knew I would get home eventually. And at least I had a home to go to.

It didn't happen very often either, because in keeping with my championship level squareness, I had a lot of hobbies: choir, orchestra (I played the trumpet, that most seductive of instruments . . .), dancing, hockey, netball, and church, of course. I had stuff going on, it just wasn't very sexy stuff. But that was also an element of Baby's character I perceived and related to strongly – it's made clear from the opening lines of the film she is interested in something other than getting men to fancy her – she is not especially seeking male attention. She's curious about everyone and everything, and I resolved to follow her example.

I've never thought it was very helpful to reduce every encounter to whether there is a presence or absence of sexual attraction. This has always been very important to me, and so Baby's attitude really struck a chord. You don't have to fancy everyone. Not everyone will fancy you. And that shouldn't matter – it's not the all-important factor that some people can make it. And it's certainly no yardstick by which to measure your worth. I think Baby's approach to this is due in part to the very secure relationship she enjoys with her father. Which in turn is why he finds it hard to adjust to her attraction to Johnny – it is so powerful that it threatens to engulf his little girl, and perhaps disturb her integrity, her essence, her principles.

But Jake has imbued Baby with a sense of herself, as distinct from what any man might think of her, and this ironically attracts Johnny. 'You're not afraid of anything,' he shouts at her, both frustrated and admiring. And it makes the sting all the more sharp when he later calls her a coward. 'I don't see you running up to Daddy, telling him I'm your guy,' he admonishes her as they come across Jake Houseman and she drags him out of sight. He realises she is ashamed of him, or that perhaps she is still a little girl in many ways – Daddy's little girl. It's not a flattering assessment and is all the more potent given that it refers back to Johnny's first insulting assessment of her – has nothing changed in the course of their time together? Yes, and no.

Giving girls the freedom to go out and find love, sex, romance, is tough for any parent. I am firmly of the 'I'd rather they were doing it under my roof than on a park bench' school of parenting, and I think that if I had been in any way sexually active as a teenager, my parents would have been too. But I was a late starter and didn't really give them too much to worry about there. Although, with that said, I tested a different set of boundaries by going on what must have been one of the first internet dates in the UK.

It's 1997, and we've got the internet at home. It resides in a PC computer, which lives in the study/spare room. It has a dial-up connection, so you can't use the landline phone while it's in use. It is charged like a phone call – minute by minute. And it has very early forms of chat rooms, via AOL.

I loved those chat rooms – I loved typing things to strangers. I loved teasing people, and pretending I was someone else, creating a character, only to abandon it and start again somewhere else. It was late-night fun – I would creep down after everyone was in bed, and chat to people I would never meet in real life, or IRL as we all call it now. Our phone bills were APPALLING, and I got in huge trouble. But I didn't stop. I couldn't. I found it addictive.

One person I 'met' was called Chris. We chatted a lot. Then suddenly we moved to emails. This was an extraordinary thing to do back then, even though it feels normal now. I told no one about it. Absolutely no one. There was no sexual stuff going on – we talked about music, TV shows, films, food and where we lived. He had a job and was a few years older than me. Then one night he suggested we talk on the phone. And I said yes. So then we started chatting almost daily, late at night, me crouching by the phone so I could grab it at the first ring and not wake anyone up.

We never attempted to define this relationship, but there was clearly some chemistry. The idea that we would meet started to enter the atmosphere, unspoken at first, and then suddenly without warning, an invitation came. He had two tickets to see The Fugees at Wembley Arena. We could meet there and then he would drive me home, a journey of around 45 minutes. And I agreed. Can you believe it? I still can't. It was an insane-sounding thing to do back then. It's more normal now, but there's still a stigma attached to 'meeting someone online', even though almost all of us do it. But back then, it didn't exist. If you joined a dating agency, you went to their office, and filled out a paper form, and they would call you on the phone if they found a match. Going on a date with someone you have met through the computer literally had no frame of reference in 1997. It made about as much sense as going out for dinner with your toaster. It didn't happen. But I said yes. And still, I told no one.

Except for my dad. On the day of the concert. Now, I could have lied – I was 18, and it was perfectly normal for me to go out for an evening and come home late. There were loads of ways I could have covered it. But I think I suddenly felt the chill of danger. I realised that what I was about to do was at best, a bit risky, at worst, totally reckless. He could kill me. He could kill me in the car and then dump my body on the A40. I did not know this man. I didn't even know what he looked like – there was no way an ordinary person could easily get a photo of themselves to send on email back then. It didn't seem to matter. All I knew was that we made each other laugh. I think in some way I trusted that more than anything.

My dad was quite calm about it.

'I'm not going to tell Mum,' he said, 'she'll worry.' And she would, quite rightly.

'Dad, there's a man I met on this internet,' I had started.

'The what?' 'The internet – the World Wide Web.'

'Ah, yes . . .'

'Yes, and we've been talking in a chat room . . .'

'A what?'

'It's like a digital . . . like a digital . . .' Like a digital what? We don't have chat rooms in real life, we have pubs, but these aren't like pubs. They're not like anything.

'It's like a virtual space you can talk to other people . . .'

'Is he a real person?'

'Yes.'

'How do you know?' Good point, but I had an answer.

'We've spoken on the phone. Quite a lot.' It was at this point I realised how far it had gone. And how much I had concealed.

'OK . . .'

'OK, and . . . and he's asked me to go to a concert with him. Tonight. At Wembley.'

'Right. How are you getting home?'

'He's going to drive me . . .'

'OK. Thanks for telling me, I appreciate it.'

And that was it. I could go. Astonishing. ASTONISHING. But also great, because you know what? Statistically, that man was not going to rape me, or kill me. I know the problems in the world are many, and life is not always a safe space for women, but still, how to balance the likelihood of danger against the thrill of opportunity? It's a tough question, and we ask it of ourselves over and over again. Baby asks it of herself. Her father asks it of himself and his daughter. Frightened by the risk she has taken by immersing herself in the life of these dancers she barely knows, and seeing his daughter in full make-up for the first time, Jake Houseman shouts, 'I don't want you seeing those people ever again. And wash that stuff off your face.'

But having mitigated the risk as much as I could, I went to the concert. I went to meet Chris. He could be The One, I thought. We have this amazing connection online, and on the phone. We could be together forever.

He was waiting for me outside the tube station. I saw him before he saw me. And . . . and . . . oh god, I felt it straight away in the pit of my stomach – a queasiness, a certain knowledge. I knew there and then that . . . I didn't fancy him at all. Not one bit. And the moment he clocked me, I could see in his eyes that he didn't fancy me either. There was nothing wrong with either of us, it just wasn't there. It was good on the phone, but the chemistry, the pheromones, the whatever, were nowhere to be seen now. They say you know in the first ten seconds whether you are physically attracted to someone, and if it's not there, it's almost impossible to manufacture. The disappointment was huge, but also there was some sense of relief. Because I wasn't really looking for a boyfriend. I was about to go to university.

Chris was the perfect gentleman. He really couldn't have been nicer. We enjoyed The Fugees and then he drove me home in his silver Mercedes. As we pulled up outside the house, there was a light on. I knew I was being waited up for. I didn't have a mobile phone – no one did – so parents just had to wait and worry. I thanked Chris for a lovely evening, and he said the same. And I went into the house, and we never spoke to or saw each other ever again.

Years later – 12 years, to be exact – I repeated my actions almost exactly, though now there was Broadband, Wi-Fi enabled mobile phones and social media. I met a man through Facebook, we started chatting online, we moved to the phone, and then I agreed to go to Liverpool to meet him. I booked a hotel for the weekend. I was now 30, but I still told my dad what I was doing, and he nodded – we'd been here before. I had form. I said to only worry if he hadn't heard from me by Monday. And then I completely forgot to text him because I was having such a good time. Monday came and went, and still, I did not text. You know what's worse? He texted me and I DIDN'T EVEN REPLY. A monumentally inconsiderate way to behave. Later, my dad revealed that he was unsure whether to leave me to it or call the police. A tough choice. He left me to it, though he knew nothing about the man I was with. And I'm glad he did. Reader, I married him.

Letting go of your children is hard, but *Dirty Dancing* provides an interesting template. Johnny gets a pretty severe brush-off from Baby's father when he goes to try and make peace. He wants to thank the doctor for helping Penny, and it has clearly taken some courage to walk up to the cabin door and knock on it. But the meeting ends badly as Jake makes it clear he thinks Johnny was the one to get Penny 'in trouble', and Johnny is too proud to correct him. But later, when this dancer with a life so strange and alien to the Housemans, returns to find her, and discovers she has been put in a corner away from the action, with the implication that it is Jake who has put her there, by accident or design, Johnny is not having it. That line, 'Nobody puts Baby in a corner', says, 'Let this young woman show what she can be – don't stifle her potential through fear and prejudice'. It was utterly thrilling when I was young, and still is.

Then, when Johnny lifts Baby high above his head, so everyone can see how she has changed, how she has become a woman, Jake Houseman, her father, can't help but feel what we feel. 'When I'm wrong, I say I'm wrong,' he admits to Johnny, before turning to his youngest daughter with tears in his eyes and says, 'You looked wonderful out there.' Not a dry eye in the house.

The urge to protect young girls is strong, and with

good reason, but life isn't as terrifying as we think it is, and we should not put them in corners because of some notion that it is for their own protection. The hardest thing for me to do with my step-daughter was convey that even though there could be a rapist on every corner, at every party, there probably isn't. And with a few basic safety checks in place, she should proceed through life as if there isn't. It's either that, or miss everything. I'm not trying to be glib, or deny reality – I've had my own #MeToo moments of varying severity. But I have recovered and I still want adventure sometimes. Baby wants to experience it all, and she doesn't stop to look too hard first. So I say, be more Baby. I think it's worth the risk.

5
You Don't Own Me

I knew within the first couple of hours of arriving at Oxford University that I had made a mistake. I had been nervous, of course, like any new student, but I had stoically told myself in the days leading up to the first day of term that everybody would be in the same boat – we would all be wandering around in an unfamiliar environment, hoping to meet new people, tender stems suddenly feeling our way in a larger pot.

With my dad's help, I unloaded my stuff from the car to my new room, waved him off, and now I was properly alone. With butterflies in my stomach, I forced myself out into the bright October sunshine to do that most dreaded of things, 'make new friends'.

It was about half an hour after I had crossed the quad multiple times, trying to look fascinating yet approachable, casual yet intriguing, that I noticed lots of my fellow freshers were already in groups of three or more, and many of them seemed to walk with a purpose that I couldn't fathom. Where were they going, with such confidence? How had they made these friendships so quickly, that seemed to ring with easy shared laughter?

I tagged along behind three shrieking girls to eavesdrop on their conversation. It took me a minute to realise that they were discussing dinner plans.

'I said we'd meet Olly in the Kings Arms at six, and he's bringing Rufus and Jonty – thought we'd get a curry at Shimla Pinks or something.'

'OK, yah, cool. I hope Olly doesn't bring his cousin – haven't seen him since I vommed on his jacket at Kitty's parents, silver wedding thing last summer.'

Oh. Ohhh. Ohhhhhhh, I see. I suddenly felt so, so stupid. Of course. Of course, of course, of course. They all knew each other already. They'd all gone to the same ten schools. They all went skiing together. They all had thousands and thousands of cousins who had also gone to the same ten schools. And now they were all here. And they had dinner plans. I retreated into the shadow of the imposing chapel to calm down and plot my next move.

It was then that I started to panic. I envisaged three desolate years alone, wandering the medieval streets of Oxford, nose pressed to the glass of the various pubs and restaurants, forlornly watching all the Veronicas and Venetias, the Arthurs and the Harrys laughing gaily and spending their magnificent trust funds together, while I pathetically tried to make friends by pretending I also split my time between west London and the country, and knew what the fuck an 'Ile Flottante' was when it was at home.

Of course, in the end it wasn't like that. I found people, plenty of people, like me and unlike me, and I made friends for life. I tried everything (yes, everything . . .) including, but not limited to: women's rugby, rowing, comedy, drama, the Pacific Rim society (it's fusion cooking – don't be disgusting), the Christian Union, the Islamic Union, debating and the College Ball Committee. And that's just the legal stuff. There was also the notorious Piers Gaveston party (mainly lots of posh people who are now MPs taking speed in a field, wondering if they're going get any al fresco sex later), ball crashing and any number of debauched, drunken nights followed by humiliating hours in front of my tutors, empty-handed again. In the end, I had the time of my life, I really did. It was just a little bumpy to begin with, while I figured this strange new world out.

And I'm not painting myself as some kind of impover-ished working-class heroine who had never seen a building with four walls, a roof and a functioning toilet before. No, I was very all right by average standards. But this was the first time I had been amongst the truly posh. I'm from a middle-class family, but the trouble with being middle class is that nobody wants to admit it. So I'm saying it now. I am firmly middle class. But I went to a local comprehensive, rather than a grammar school, or one of the cheaper private schools, and so I had had a different experience of education than even many of the other middle-class kids who got a place at Oxford that year. I spoke differently, punctuating my chat with liberal use of the ubiquitous Watford phrase 'd'y'knarr'I'mean' to such an extent that certain boys used to shout it at me across the dining hall to take the piss out of my flattish, estuary-ish twang.

The irony was some kids back home thought I was posh because we had books in the house and I could play the piano (very, very badly. No, really – very, very badly. I'm not being modest. People sometimes think I'm being modest and make me play it, and then afterwards they look embarrassed because they have to agree with me about how bad I am). I dressed a little differently at first too – I remember in the first week of term, putting on my prized shiny black Adidas tracksuit trousers with the white stripes down each leg (they cost a whole weekend's pay working in Martin's newsagent), strolling into the common room with the swagger of an England under-21s footballer and enduring a second-year student simply pointing at them and laughing in a high-pitched squealy way that I assume is usually reserved for occasions such as putting horse manure in other boys' beds in the dorm, or whatever it is these people do at boarding school for fun. Oh, the mortification! I had got it wrong, whatever 'it' was. I bought myself some dark denim boot-cut jeans pretty sharpish – this was 1997, after all. I would have to adapt fast.

One of the things I learned from the posh people, now I had a chance to observe them up close, is that it's not cool to appear to be trying very hard. Actually, I will say they have that in common with some of the people I was at school with – who were very firmly at the other end of the social spectrum – although with rather different results because those kids didn't end up at Oxford, even though many of them were far cleverer than plenty who do get a place. It's just the support isn't there, or the money, the good word from a teacher to their old buddy at Wotnot College. This still goes on. But we middle classes, we sometimes manage to kick through the partition because we are born to try, and although we can't necessarily expect to be given everything on a silver platter, we have seen enough of the good stuff to know we want it, and that if we push hard enough we may just be able to get more of it for ourselves.

We middle-class girls are often described as pushy, grabby and greedy, along with bossy, aggressive and difficult. We are associated with taking what we want, rather than waiting to be given it (clue: the gift isn't coming, not for us – we realise that early on. We're going to have to get it ourselves). And kiss goodbye to being cool – forget it. But we will get that sense of deep satisfaction that comes with achieving something, anything, on our own terms, eventually. That is quite precious, and something all middle-class success stories share.

The middle is the only class you can join via your own efforts, too – it seems that members of the 'working class' or 'upper class' insist that you are only a true member by birth. But we middle classes aren't so exclusive – you want something badly? Are you unafraid to show it? Then welcome, my upstart brothers and sisters – a gravel driveway can be yours if you just put the hours in. I've had a fantastically vulgar but expensive and highly covetable hot tub plumbed into my garden – come on in, the water is literally lovely.

Those of us born into middle class-dom know we're lucky, because we were probably fairly comfortable growing up. And again, there's nothing cool about being comfortable, which is why anyone with artistic pretentions likes to empha-sise the traumas and the discomfort, even if they're transpar-ently non-existent. Because truthfully, we had a good start, courtesy of our parents. But there still came a time where we broke away and had to learn the hard way, gaining experience, working on a Saturday for money, doing shit-awful jobs that kick your soul to death while co-workers laugh at our naively stated ambitions to 'become a writer' (I tried this once when I briefly worked as a dinner lady in a local school. You could've cut the silence with one of their very blunt knives. Then the laughing started. I was put on washing-up for the rest of the week to remind me of my proper place – fair enough, I was being quite annoying). The posh and rich never get to do all that, and I saw many of them fail later because of it. Of all the people I went to university with who later went into the tricky creative industries, the ones who are still hanging on, just about making a living, are broadly working class ones (who had to push so hard to get there in the first place, they're not stopping for anyone now) and we the middle-class ones, trying, trying, trying.

So, trying hard is not cool, but it has its own rewards. As much as I watched the leggy Veronicas coolly smoking a Marlboro Light and swishing their lovely long hair, and envied them the ease with which everything seemed to fall into their laps, I knew I could never be one of them. I was a Baby. I can try to look like I don't care, but the fact is I do,

I really, really do. And nothing ever falls into my lap, apart from Spaghetti Bolognese off a typically over-loaded fork. So I would have to work for it. And sometimes that makes a woman seem charmless.

'She's very ambitious' is almost considered an insult in some quarters of British life, but I admit that I was. I am. I am very ambitious. It makes me flinch a little to say it because I know you are supposed to act as if everything is a lovely surprise, but as far as I can see, only wealthy white men get to act like that, to say 'I've been very lucky', because, well, yes, you are very lucky, so perhaps it *is* all a lovely surprise. As for the rest of us, we know exactly how it's all happened because we were there every single, painful step of the way. You'll never hear J.K. Rowling pretending to be surprised by her success at a dinner party. You'll never hear Serena Williams saying, 'Gosh, I suppose I've just been very lucky.' You'll never hear Michelle Obama smirking smugly, 'I don't really know what I'm doing, but don't tell anyone', before winking over her glass of champagne as if it's all impossibly charming. No. They all know exactly how they got where they got. Every gruelling moment is burned on their brains.

And so to *Dirty Dancing*, and the issues of class and politics it raises. Although it's not the first thing people think of when they remember the film, it's all in there, bubbling away under the surface, and popping up in some unexpected ways. In her brilliant essay, '*Dirty Dancing* is the greatest movie of all time' for the website Jezebel.com, journalist Irin Carmon makes a startling point about our heroine, Baby Houseman:

Told her whole life that she could do anything and change the world, she's faced with the hypocrisy of a long-shunned minority enacting its own unexamined exclusion, this time on class grounds. The guests at Kellerman's look comfortable, but they were raised in the Depression and traumatized by World War II. She can contrast the welcome her family received at the resort with the chilly, dismissive one Johnny and his working-class dance crew gets. She can dance with the owner's son and thaw a little when she learns he's going freedom riding with the bus boys, then see how he treats Johnny. She can find out that the supposed prize, Yale Medical School and out-WASPing-the-WASPs Robbie, is also an Ayn Rand-reading cad whose life philosophy is, 'Some people count, some people don't.[1]

There's a lot to unpack in this statement. First, I have to admit that I would estimate for my first hundred or so viewings of *Dirty Dancing*, I had no idea the Housemans are a Jewish family. I did not understand that Max Kellerman's hotel is supposed to be part of a group of resorts in the Catskills, an area that was a popular holiday spot with Jewish families in the mid-twentieth century. In many ways, this doesn't matter at all – ignorance of it doesn't stop you understanding and enjoying the story. But it was interesting to discover later in my life that screenwriter Eleanor Bergstein said of her film, 'It's a Jewish movie . . . if you know what you're looking at.'

This is startling, because the film is set in 1963. Let's say Baby's parents are 40-ish, meaning they were both born in the early 1920s. They lived through the Holocaust – as in, the knowledge of it – and so did every other middle-aged person at Kellerman's Resort. We don't have to assume they were immigrants fleeing Nazi Europe, but they will have had family there or known people who did. Max Kellerman is older still, and his friend, the band leader Tito Suarez, will also have seen great hardship. I don't mean to kill the mood, but somehow this gives everything a rather different sensibility. All these people have worked hard to get to this place of comfort, and they are protective of it, and each other. Poverty is very much in living memory. As Max says to Tito as the season comes to a close, 'You and me, Tito, we've seen it all – Bubbe and Zayde serving the first pasteurized milk to the boarders – through the war years, when we didn't have any meat – through the Depression, when we didn't have anything.'

Furthermore, it has been pointed out many times that though the guests at Kellerman's are affluent Jewish families, the dancers almost all appear to be white, working-class kids with difficult backgrounds. There are but two black dancers who seem only to dance with each other, which always strikes me as a bit backward, but I'm not going to argue that *Dirty Dancing* is in any way a representative film of African-Americans. It is a significant blind spot.

But the film does focus on the financial problems of the dancers, who are presumably not paid a fortune for their talent and trouble. You will have noticed the naked fear both Penny and Johnny display at the idea of getting fired – they have no cushion, this is it, and it's a good gig. They are willing to risk everything in order to preserve this job, including health and humiliation. The importance of work is rammed home to Baby with Johnny's stinging response to her innocent question about Penny missing the dance at the Sheldrake, 'Can't somebody else fill in?'

'No, Miss Fix-it. Somebody else can't "fill in". Maria has to work all day. She can't learn the routines. And Janet has to fill in for Penny. Everybody works here.'

The emphasis and meaning is clear – 'You are a privileged middle-class child, and you have no idea what our lives are like'.

I am not the first to point out that part of Jake Houseman's fear and disapproval of Johnny Castle comes not just from his snaky-hips and soft little pout, but also that he is not a nice Jewish boy from a nice Jewish family. He represents something different and dangerous. He is not the kind of man that is suitable for Baby. These kids who get themselves 'in trouble' and have to visit backstreet abortionists are not the kind of friends Jake Houseman wants for his daughter. He has paid thousands of dollars in hard-earned cash for Baby's education, and she's not going to throw her life away on this. They frighten him, too – they seem reckless.

So, Baby comes from a self-made middle-class family. We don't know the background of her parents, but let's assume they are not of Rothschild stock. Her father is a doctor; he has not inherited his wealth. He has worked hard to get where he is (Kellerman's) – as his wife points out at the very beginning, 'This is his first real vacation in six years' – and yet has not lost his liberal views. He must have given Baby some sense of moral responsibility – she is too young to have reached all her conclusions herself. And it would seem from one throwaway remark that he and Marge have not always had it so easy – he gently chides his older daughter, Lisa, as she fusses and flaps about dresses and shoes she has left at home. Baby joins in, mockingly comparing Lisa's complaints to a list of actual catastrophes – 'Monks burning themselves in protest' – burnishing her right-on values as she glows in the reflected approval of her father. She is proud to be aware of the suffering of others, and she even feels confident she can help fix it. Perhaps there is even a smidge of virtue signalling here? Baby likes to draw the distinction between herself and Lisa. If the film were made now, she would be the woke one of the family.

She later tells Neil Kellerman, a capitalist in sports casual clothing, she is about to start studying 'economics of under-developed countries' as her major in college. To underline the point even further, as they arrive at the hotel, she is reading a book called *The Plight of the Peasant*, and then makes a show of helping the porter to unload the car. Thus, she unknowingly begins her journey to Johnny, as the porter is Billy, Johnny's cousin (and deliverer of watermelons to sexy parties). He thanks her, and quips, 'Hey, you want a job here?' Not a job, Billy, no – the sexual experience of a lifetime, please, thank you.

The first ten minutes of the film are absolutely packed with subtle, and not so subtle, class markers, where Bergstein sets out her stall, and lets us know where everybody stands. Even Marge's line at dinner that night about sending their left-over food to 'starving children in Europe' seems less silly when you consider her age and the era. She is corrected by Baby – 'Try South-East Asia, Ma' – but the concern is still there. It's a neat little joke about that type of vague middle-class concern for people 'out there having a hard time', and it still feels fresh now. Or think about the 'woke rich' attending philanthropic lunches that cost $10,000 per table, which are really 'see and be seen' networking events, where nobody quite knows what they're raising money for.

Baby is aware of her privilege, and aware of class warfare. She even goes a little gooey-eyed over Penny, who describes the tough life she has led – 'Is this part of the artistic vocation?', you can almost see her wondering, like many a middle-class girl before her. Am I too comfortable to really understand, or achieve what these people have? Baby's tin-eared response to Penny's grumpy sign-off that she didn't even care when she was thrown out by her mother, aged 16, because she only ever wanted to be a dancer, is 'I envy you'. It is delivered in such a naively simpering tone you can hardly blame the dancer's twisted grimace of a laugh as she snaps the clasps on the wig box shut with the force of a fired bullet.

But that classic middle-class romanticising of the struggling artist is hard to break for Baby, and you can see her thinking, 'If only my parents would throw me out, even for a couple of weeks, perhaps I will achieve the level of grit and determination it takes to get from the street to here' – which is essentially supervising the slightly odd pastime of 'trying on wigs' by a luxury boating lake, and teaching old people how to merengue in a gazebo all summer. Baby doesn't 'envy'

Penny at all, and Penny knows it, even if she herself doesn't. It's nothing like the life Baby will get for herself. But it's as much as Penny will ever have, even with the hard work, commitment and talent she has put in. Because Baby is middle class and Penny isn't. Even as it's painful to see Baby slapped down, I love Penny for refusing to be patronised here.

But the anger and energy of these new people excite her – she's not the first middle-class girl to get a thrill from the fury and relentless drive of a person with nowhere else to go, and she certainly won't be the last. As she gazes up at Johnny, balancing on his log, telling her the story of his route into the dance world, she is romanticising for all she is worth. It's only later, at a point of tension between them, that the reality of his life, his options or lack of them, properly gets through, and I would say it's this moment that she stops just fancying him, and starts falling in love. As he paces uphill following an altercation with Max Kellerman's grandson, Neil, with the threat of a sacking hanging over him, he finally lays it out for her. If he fails at this, it's back home to join the family business as a painter and decorator. All the talent, all the passion, will mean nothing – there is no trust fund, no 'flat in town' to stay in, no wealthy relative with contacts in the theatre world.

As Johnny says earlier, with genuine fear and anguish in his voice, 'I'm balancing on shit here, and quick as that I can be back down there again.' Back to obscurity, back to hard labour, back to knowing your place, back to having your dreams crushed. It's a line that hits home because it's so real. I should think Eleanor Bergstein felt that way a few times in her life. Perhaps Jake Houseman knows all about it too, but ironically, he has worked so hard to protect his wife and children from any insecurity, he barely recognises a kindred spirit when he sees one, instead placing his approval on the creepy Robbie, who reads Ayn Rand for fun. And props to Eleanor Bergstein for that one – I can't name another romantic musical drama with an Ayn Rand gag in it, but I'm open to being corrected. 'Some people count; some people don't,' Robbie says, as he slaps down his well-thumbed copy of *The Fountainhead*. If Baby thought he was going to do the decent thing, as the father of Penny's baby, and pay for her termination, she was living in a different world. Robbie even thinks she will understand – they are both middle class – but Baby pours a jug of water into his lap. Rand's ultra right-wing bodice ripper is unlikely to sit easily on the shelf alongside her copy of *The Plight of the Peasant*, it would seem (even though *The Plight of the Peasant* doesn't actually exist).

In fact, it's Robbie who makes the crudest class reference of all, slut-shaming Baby, Penny and Lisa all in one, while at the same time insulting Johnny and all the other dancers: 'Don't worry, Baby, I went slumming too,' he says of his affair with Penny, before getting lamped by our boy in black. And he deserves it. But the meaning is clear – the dancers are slum dwellers – sexy slum dwellers, but slum dwellers nonetheless. You bang them once, and then move on.

When I was at university, I went on a couple of dates with a boy whose father I met one night over dinner. The relationship didn't last, and I later found out that dear Pater had told his son that I was not the sort of girl he should marry.

They were a pretty well-to-do family, and I think there was some suspicion that my parents were '*Guardian* readers'. Certainly, my schooling didn't pass muster, and though I could be congratulated on showing initiative in 'dragging myself up to Oxford', there was the overwhelming sense that I would be trouble, and broke trouble at that.

He was probably not altogether wrong, and I hope the boy is now happily married to someone more suitable than me. The journalist Tanya Gold brilliantly referred to a similar experience she had had, of discovering that for a certain class of boy (and their fathers) she would always be a 'girl for now, not a girl for later'. The line was taken from Laura Wade's play *Posh* (later, a feature film, *Riot Club*) about the notorious Bullingdon Club (a drinking and destruction society for rich boys at Oxford, of which George Osborne, Boris Johnson and David Cameron were all members). As Gold recalled in her piece for the *Sunday Times*:

> *A [Bullingdon Club]) member says in the play that there are 'girls for now and girls for later'. When I was at Oxford University, my husband says, someone used this very phrase about me. I was apparently 'a girl for now', which is probably better than being 'a girl for later', if your 'later' is a lifetime with a sub-Bullingdon cartoon.*[2]

But even if we 'girls for now' ultimately escape the fate of a stultifying aristo-marriage, the shock of finding that you, a nice, hard-working, middle-class girl, are not good enough (no family money, no titles, no entry in Debrett's, thighs wider than your calves) is quite choking. But Johnny, as our working-class hero, sees it coming. He knows he can never quite rely on the kindness of strangers, hence his initial spiky reaction to Baby's offer of help, and his instant cold fury and contempt when he sees so clearly that she is ashamed to introduce him to her father. Johnny does not take kindly to being a 'girl for now', and this is how Baby suddenly makes him feel. The battle isn't over yet, not by a long way.

But smug, privileged Robbie gets his comeuppance when Johnny comes at him – there's a proper tussle to the ground, before Johnny controls his temper, parting with the words, 'You're not worth it.' And he isn't. It's not something you can imagine Neil Kellerman doing, and this physicality is brought to the screen by Bergstein to underline his background – he comes from a place where if words fail, and someone needs to be taught a lesson, you sometimes have to use your fists. And he is defending two important women – Baby and Penny – one of whom is lying ill in the room next door as a result of Robbie's callousness. It doesn't faze Baby. In fact, I think she quite likes it. She certainly isn't put off as she wraps her arms around his head, while Robbie scarpers.

It's Penny who issues the most heartfelt warning shot as she lies recovering from her abortion. Clocking the tension between Baby and Johnny, and this not being her first time at the rodeo, she leans in to her old friend and dance partner and says urgently, 'You've got to stop it. Now.' Johnny looks ashen and ashamed – caught in the act. When I was a kid, I didn't fully grasp the problem. Yes, Max Kellerman has said the dance staff shouldn't fraternise with the 'daughters of guests' – yet another class division here, as he positively encourages his waiting staff to romance them, but then they are 'nice Jewish boys' who go to Yale and Harvard and only work here to earn a little extra cash for college treats like Robbie's Alfa Romeo – but I didn't see why it was so serious. I didn't see why losing the Sheldrake gig was such a big deal either. It's explained of course, that they would prefer not to lose it because of the extra income, but I foolishly did not relate to that sense of the dream being over if they have to go back home. It's this job, or nothing.

And they are at the mercy of a boss who doesn't especially like or respect these 'entertainers', who have questionable morals and unsupportive families. Kellerman's is all about wholesome families who look after each other. The dancers are a necessary evil who get themselves in trouble and can't be trusted.

It's only after 20 years working in the entertainment world that I full appreciate the fear of losing a job because of personal reasons – many's the time I have done a gig when I should have been hiding under a duvet, simply because I couldn't afford to drop it, or didn't want to be labelled difficult or unreliable. It gives you a sort of toughness that isn't necessarily normal or good for you.

This kind of class struggle is played out often in stories of all kinds, but it is unusual to see it take place where middle-class Jewish families are the ones with privilege, who are in charge. Eleanor Bergstein experienced it all first-hand, as she holidayed in the Catskills with her middle-class Jewish family but then went on to become a dancer herself, leaving the

safety of the traditional professions behind – doctor/lawyer/
whatever. It's a unique perspective, but she has catapulted it
into the mainstream and made it a universal story nonetheless.

Nobody watches *Dirty Dancing* as a film about an
ambitious, rich Jewish girl who has a mad affair with a gen-
tile boy from the wrong side of the tracks, but in Bergstein's
mind I think that is a big part of it. It's about how dancing
can transcend all these barriers and become a universal
language. Dancing can heal rifts and show us a deeper
experience of being human. Jake Houseman's emotional
'You looked wonderful out there' declaration to a tearful
post-lift Baby and a triumphant Johnny is the olive branch
across the divide. He finally understands – maybe he has even
reconnected with some part of himself he lost along the way.
His wife, Marge 'I think she gets this from me' Houseman,
definitely understands.

Once again, here is that motif: if you dance with your
heart, you can be trusted – which is almost Bergstein's
motto. Dancing is free, and money doesn't necessarily equate
to morality.

This is where the distinction lies, and why, although
Eleanor Bergstein herself said it is a 'Jewish film', it also has
universal appeal. In many ways, *Dirty Dancing* is a story
about people who have money, property and family versus
those who don't. The families at the Catskills, the owners of
the hotels (note how important it is for Max Kellerman that
his grandson Neil is going to take over) and even the waiting
staff have these things. The dancers don't. These are the two
tribes. But ultimately, it's the hypocrisy of the wealthy that

is shown up by the humble honesty of the poor (a classic storyline). It's all very satisfying, and appeals to our sense of justice. The Houseman family are not wholly bad, and neither is Max Kellerman, but they have made assumptions about Johnny and the dancers that are wrong, and Baby is there to show them their error.

Johnny has a good heart, that's the main thing. He is decent, even though he has to deal with prejudice constantly. The burgeoning trust Johnny displays in Baby is one of the most touching aspects of the film, and it's why he is an enduring romantic lead. He changes himself as much as he changes her, and vice versa. They make each other better, which is a very appealing journey to watch.

This journey comes about, mainly, because Baby walks into a different world with an open mind, an open heart, and yes, open legs, but she emerges a better, stronger, wiser woman. You have to meet people who are not like you in order to understand the world, and have true empathy and compassion. Baby is the living embodiment of this. She's earned those orgasms.

More widely, the film is set during a time of immense political and social upheaval, with JFK in the White House (though not for very much longer), Martin Luther King leading the civil rights movement (though not for very much longer), women and other minority groups demanding equality, the Vietnam War on the horizon, changes in musical tastes, and attitudes to sex. This is surely deliberate – the old orders are being challenged on every level and change is in the air. Baby is about to live through one of the biggest cultural shifts of the previous hundred years. There's rock 'n' roll playing in the family car as they drive to Kellerman's, and on the various record players that are shown throughout the film. In the end, even mountain stalwart Max Kellerman has to concede that the world he knew no longer exists, and in order to stay in business, he will have to adapt. And suddenly, there in front of him, grinding their hips together, is the future. Get on, or get left behind. Ultimately, the Catskills did get left behind, but this perfectly preserved moment in time, played out in the safety of a luxury resort, gives us a little flavour of how it might have felt.

Love across the class divide is a great story to tell. Rich people being humbled by poor people is another. When you bring these two together, you have cinematic dynamite – it's *Dr Zhivago* meets *A Christmas Carol*, but with more mambo and sequins. Stir in some unforgettable choreography, spice it with one of the sexiest seduction scenes of all time (she seduces *him*, remember?) and you can't fail.

These lessons went deep into me when I was watching as a young teenager. Later, when I was made to feel small or belittled, because in the poshest environment in the world I was deemed by some as not quite up to scratch, I think *Dirty Dancing* kept me going. I thought of Baby. I thought of Johnny. These things didn't really matter, I felt. I could walk around feeling a bit smug that I knew a secret – that I was the middle-class girl hero of my own story, and one day, if I stuck up for myself and what I believed in, worked as hard as I could, and didn't judge anyone on first appearances, I would get all the good stuff. Along with some excellent sex. I'm proud to say that I have indeed got some of it. I feel confident the rest will surely come. Because I'm a middle-class square who tries too hard, and doesn't know when to give up – just like Baby. And perhaps, so are you. There are worse things to be. We get shit done. Baby teaches us not to feel intimidated by the unknown, or close ourselves off to people who seem different to us.

Surely one of the main messages of *Dirty Dancing* is just dive in and see what happens. It could be wonderful.

6
In the Still of the Night

*B*aby was my hero – have I mentioned that at all . . .? She was the one I identified with, who I found relatable. I saw everything through Baby's eyes, as many of us did, and do – we are meant to, it's constructed this way on purpose. Although shout-out to anyone who watches *Dirty Dancing* from the perspective of Vivian Pressman or Marge Houseman – perhaps these characters become more relevant to us as we get older . . .

But if you wanted serious, shiny, 'I want that body, and that hair, and that face, and that everything', it was all about Penny. Penny was aspirational. Penny was Jane Fonda doing aerobics. Penny was Pamela Anderson in *Baywatch*. Penny was the 1980s dream, and even though she was supposed to exist 20 years earlier, she was the 1987 fantasy look all over. Penny dazzled me – I dreamed of being Penny, except without the traumatic termination of a pregnancy. The dresses are spectacular, but even the downtime wear is great.

But beyond the dazzle, Penny's story is the challenge of the film. It's the substance too; it's what gives the whole thing some proper gravitas. It shows a middle stage of womanhood that is so often unrepresented, ignored, trivialised, or suppressed with endless daily concerns of motherhood. If Baby is the ingénue, and Vivian is the cautionary tale, Penny is the meat in the sandwich, so to speak. Penny has a genuine mess to attend to, and frankly, let's be honest, we've all had our scares. Despite her immense glamour, Penny is in fact the 'everywoman'. She's all of us, hiding inside the most perfect shell.

Now, I'm not going to pretend I understood all of it at first, though Penny's woes have increased in resonance as I have got older. But at the age of 11, and without anything being explicitly explained in the trickier parts of the film, there was room for confusion. I admit that I didn't quite follow the Penny storyline.

When she is first discovered by Baby crying in the resort kitchen, hiding under a stainless-steel unit, I honestly thought she was upset because she was hungry and couldn't find any food in the apparently empty and spotless kitchen. Then for a while I wondered if perhaps she was stuck under the unit itself and couldn't get out? Or had she possibly suddenly lost the use of her legs, which for a dancer, I reasoned, would indeed be traumatic. Or anyone, in fact. And given that when Johnny arrives to help, he picks her up and carries her away in his arms, it seemed like a viable theory. But no – she dances again only a day later in the film, so that can't be it. It is explained in the next scene that she was 'knocked up', but god only knew what that meant. Beaten up, perhaps? Fired?

Then it seems she must go away for a bit and this will cost money, and she comes back very ill. Now, I knew that consumption could be an extremely serious illness – I had heard about it in *Jane Eyre* – and so when Penny, shivering and feverish on her bed, seemed to be exhibiting symptoms of TB, I feared the worst.

Why she needed money, I didn't know – had she visited another man and caught a cold? And why Baby's doctor father was so appalled by it all was a mystery to me. Why be so angry with Johnny about it? He couldn't help it if Penny had caught a bad chest infection, could he? And what was all this talk of a dirty knife? Had she been in a fight? It all seemed odd, and had nothing to do with the dancing.

Later, we are told Penny can still have children after her illness, which I was obviously pleased for her about, but I couldn't see the relevance. I mulled it over for some time, and concluded there was something else going on, something extra that I wasn't getting. But I surmised that it all hinged around this mysterious but charged phrase, 'knocked up'.

Initial enquiries at school with my friends drew a blank. We had no idea. I thought I might ask a teacher, but something held me back. Similarly, at home, I wasn't sure this was something to bring up over soup and sandwiches at lunchtime. I wanted to get the full *Dirty Dancing* experience though, and so I had to know. Finally, I hit upon the genius plan of asking my former babysitter, now aged 19, and well versed in the ways of men, what 'knocked up' meant. I knew she would know because she had brought her boyfriend round once when babysitting the younger me and my little sister, and they had made funny noises from the living room when they were supposed to be watching *Dead Poets Society* and waiting for my parents to get home. She would definitely know. And she did. AND I WAS SHOCKED.

Oh shit, this *Dirty Dancing* film is WAY deeper than I thought. Knocked up meant PREGNANT. And Penny had had an ABORTION. Which was a subject we were about to cover in R.E. for our ethical debate, and I was unsure of my feelings about it. I was going to have to look at this thing a whole different way. Poor, poor Penny. And Baby's dad, and Johnny, and the money she borrowed, and the rusty knife, and I was going to be sick. And the worst of it was, I couldn't watch it again with this new vista of understanding widening at a rate of an inch a minute because this was the point at which my VHS copy was broken. I had to just play it through in my head, scenes now shifting in focus and meaning. It certainly informed my views in our subsequent R.E. debate, where, awash with emotion and empathy for Penny, I displayed a level of apparently first-hand knowledge that I think my teacher found startling.

I have never had an abortion, but I wouldn't ever rule it out either, if I had to. Due to a condition I have had since puberty, PCOS (polycystic ovary syndrome), getting pregnant is not that easy for me and I have to try really, really hard to make it happen, which isn't always a hardship (wink, etc.). So, in many ways, I am lucky not to be one of those women who can use a man's toothbrush on the wrong day of the month, and end up with two lines on a stick. I always felt very sorry for those women – I could blithely miss a pill or two, or deal with a split condom, and pretty much guarantee that there would be no accidental baby. It's not a dilemma I am likely to face. And I'm not trying to get pregnant now, or probably will ever again, so I can't see how it would ever arise. But nevertheless, I think about the issue, as we all do, and I am pro-choice all the way. Sometimes the debate seems to centre around how people 'feel' about terminating a pregnancy, as if some people like it and some people don't, and that's the argument. But I have never met anyone who 'likes' the idea of abortion.

The only question is, should women have the legal right to an abortion if they need it? It doesn't matter whether anyone likes it, or how they feel about it. Sometimes it's as if anti-abortion campaigners believe women who have terminations trip into the clinic, swigging prosecco from their handbags, texting their BFF, 'Darling, you'll never guess where I am LOL'. And the idea that it's irresponsible to have an abortion has always struck me as odd – surely, given how horrible it is, it's the height of responsibility to say, 'I can't look after this baby, I'm going to have to do the decent thing and stop it before it goes any further. I am the only person who can do this, so it's my duty.' I am full of admiration for women who have made that decision. I'm thankful I've never had to.

I'm also thankful that I live in a country which currently gives women the right to have an abortion. I say 'currently' because I take nothing for granted. Eleanor Bergstein lived through a different time. In 1963, when *Dirty Dancing* is set (and when Bergstein was in her mid-twenties), abortion was still illegal in the United States, and it would be another decade until the United States Supreme Court ruling in the case Roe v. Wade changed everything and made legal, safe terminations available to American women. Currently – there are no guarantees.

So Penny has no choice but to pay for an illegal procedure. Cynthia Rhodes plays it so well – tough and desperate, vulnerable and steely, tearful and mature. One of the genius elements of the film, and the performances, is getting us to believe that Johnny would rather have sex with Baby than Penny. Sorry to be so blunt, but there it is. Even Eleanor Bergstein couldn't believe it, and she wrote the thing. In the Special Edition *Dirty Dancing* DVD commentary, Bergstein says again and again how unbelievably beautiful and graceful Cynthia Rhodes is, and how much less glam 'poor Jennifer' Grey looks next to her.

I actually became quite hysterical at the repetition of this point, but you have to applaud her honesty. How many of us 'normal women' have simply assumed any man would choose a Penny over us, any day of the week? We are conditioned to believe this from birth, and though we have made progress over the years since the film's release, and certainly since the time it was set, there is still a prevailing wind that blonde and thin is the ultimate in desirability. Penny is the fantasy woman, and fantasy women usually end up dead, or at least humbled. So all credit to Cynthia Rhodes for finding the humanity in the fantasy. And to Eleanor Bergstein for writing a fantasy woman who is neither punished for her beauty, nor elevated beyond any concerns of the flesh. The abortion storyline shows us, as girls and women watching, that shit happens to everyone.

Of course, it is also the catalyst for the whole story – without the abortion, Baby would not have to cover for Penny at the Sheldrake, and without that, she would never get to know Johnny. It's woven into the fabric of the whole thing. And Bergstein wanted to make sure as many people saw this representation as possible, without being off-putting or intimidating. In an interview with Broadly.com, she explained:

You can make a [serious] film, and only people who agree with you will see it. You can make a film about true love and wonderful music and pretty dancing and sexy people, and have in it a lovely girl who ends up with a dirty knife and a folding table screaming in the hallway, and maybe you understand it. So I was concerned to do it this way.[3]

And it is Penny's good character that saves her, rather than the way she looks. She digs in, she knows how to take responsibility for herself, she doesn't bother with Robbie again once it's clear he's not going to help – she takes it all on herself. She's even willing to do the Sheldrake gig and miss the window of opportunity for the abortion, because she doesn't want to let Johnny down or make a fuss. Penny is nails. What a woman.

And it's Baby – a 17-year-old girl, who immediately understands what she needs and tries to fix it. Her offer of help is automatic. There is zero discussion of the ethics of abortion. It is taken as read by all who know and care for Penny that it is the necessary and correct course of action. Actually, I just got chills as I wrote that, and in a good way. Johnny and

Billy are right there with her, and it only makes the men sexier and more appealing for not questioning Penny's right to do as she does – in fact, it is Billy who makes the arrangements. Even when Jake Houseman finds out, there doesn't appear to be any judgement on Penny, only concern for her health and disgust for the 'butcher' who didn't do a good job. It is an extraordinary scene – thanks mainly to the restraint in the writing, plus the powerful performances. It would be so easy for the film to lecture us at this point, or make Jake a patriarchal bogeyman, but Bergstein does neither. She just lets her characters be who they are – what they don't say is more important than what they do. It's not very feminist of me to think this way, but look, we all need a day off – men who promote and support women's rights are sexy. There's no point denying it.

The important part about it all is that Bergstein didn't want to pretend everything was easy just because they wore lovely dresses, and seemed to dance all night. The line in the interview Bergstein gave to Broadly.com that really strikes me is, 'Real people have to have abortions even as they're dancing.'[4] One of the aspects of *Dirty Dancing* that has provided unexpected comfort to me as I have grown older is its absolute resolution that the show must go on.

I know performers seem crazy sometimes, or inhuman, in the way we can pretend everything is fine and go on stage and do the act, even when the world is falling apart behind the scenes. But actually, I have always found it a relief – it's like a break from the problem. You literally can't think about it if you are in front of an audience, or on a live TV show. Of course, it all floods back the moment you come off stage, but for those brief moments, there is some respite. I have known more than one comedian do a gig the same night a parent has died. 'What else should I do? Sit at home and think about my newly dead mother?' one said, spreading his hands. 'She'd want me to work. It makes me feel better. It makes me feel useful.'

Perhaps this is shocking, but I can relate to it. And I can relate to Penny. In 2010, I became pregnant. We had been trying for a short while and I was excited, but wary because I knew with my condition it may not be straightforward. I didn't cancel any work, because I didn't want to tell anyone yet, or let anyone down. But I was in the toilet at a smart London venue during a rehearsal for an awards ceremony I was hosting that evening, when I noticed some blood. And some other lumps and bits. My first thought was, 'This isn't right.' My second thought was, 'I wonder if I can keep it to myself long enough to do the job?' It was paying a lot of money, and I didn't want to let them down at the last minute. But then the bleeding grew heavier, and I am not mad. I knew I had to call time and go to a hospital.

Having to walk into a room of strangers, where everyone is expecting you to be the jovial host – the comedian they booked, the comedian you were until about ten minutes ago – and quietly take the most senior person aside and say, 'I'm very sorry. I think I am having a miscarriage and I need to go to hospital. I don't think I will be able to host the show tonight. I'm really very sorry,' and then watch them slowly compute what you're saying, nod silently, and sit to one side as they call you a cab to the nearest A&E is not something I am looking to repeat. But I am so glad on this occasion some sensible part of my brain kicked in and said, 'No, Katy, this is not the flu, this is not a sprained ankle, this is not a recently ended relationship. You do not work through this. Go to the hospital.'

It was an early miscarriage, and I was fine. It was pretty painless, actually, and I was lucky. The bleeding lasted another couple of weeks. But what I regret is that I fulfilled every other contractual obligation I had over the course of that fortnight. There is an oft-repeated episode of a jaunty panel show I did, for example, during which, as well as enjoying the banter and the silliness (and I really was enjoying it – like I say, it took my mind off it for a while), I was also having my miscarriage. It doesn't all just drop out of you at once, there's a lot at first, and then it sort of dribbles on for a bit – and this was happening as I sat laughing along with the host and my fellow panelists. I didn't know what else to do, so I went to work.

There is an episode of a series I made about pop spoofs, where the first part of the show I made with a wildly famous boyband (at the time) was filmed when I was pregnant, and by the time we filmed the second part, ten days later, I wasn't any more – just the final drops of it now, before it became a memory. In between this and the panel show, I did a photoshoot on a see-saw – a SEE-SAW – which I had initially cancelled because I was pregnant, but now reinstated as it was 'no longer a problem' (I actually remember saying that on the phone to the photographer – yikes), or at least it wouldn't be for very much longer.

Throughout all these jobs, I kept thinking, 'Am I crazy to be doing this? Or is it OK? Should I tell someone working here that I'm actually in the middle of a miscarriage right now, or will they think I'm making a fuss?' In the end, I just warned people I might need to go to the loo more often than usual, and they didn't ask too much more. I was a runner once too, aged 18. You are the most junior member of a TV production team, who gets teas and coffees and anything else that needs fetching, and I thought about how I would have felt if I had gone into a reasonably well-known comedian's dressing room just before the show to see if they wanted a Kit-Kat or anything, and had them turn around and say, 'Thanks, darling, I'm fine, although I am having a miscarriage at the moment so I might pop via the loo on the way to the studio . . . actually, d'you know what? I think I would like that Kit-Kat after all.'

Back then, doing that runner's job, I'd have been frightened if someone said that to me. And I'd have thought they were a bit mad. I have my pride (well, most of it) and I did not want to be that well-known comedian, the subject of gossip, with people thinking I'd lost the plot a bit. So I kept quiet and did the work. Apart from anything else, I needed the money. If you don't do the gig, you don't get paid. There are many, many perks to being a freelance – no rush hour trains, 'working' from home, being able to masturbate at your desk without being arrested, eating four bacon sandwiches in one morning without the judgement and disapproval of your colleagues – but from time to time, a salary would come in handy, or a bit of sick pay, just to cover the times when you really should be on a sofa with a blanket and a bucket of chicken soup. And so I understood why Penny needed the Sheldrake gig, and was reluctant to turn it down, even in an emergency.

And all those times – the panel show, the boyband, the see-saw – I honestly thought of Penny. Penny got me through it. People often think that working in this entertainment world is easy – and to be completely honest with you, a lot of the time it is. You get looked after, you get driven around in nice cars, you are sometimes paid to effectively go on holiday with a camera. But there are times when it isn't. And I can't think of a better or more eloquent way to sum up the highs and lows of show business than, 'Real people have to have abortions even as they're dancing.' I might even get it tattooed somewhere.

In fact, it's not even just those of us who work in the precarious and insecure world of entertainment. So many people now work in the 'gig economy', or are forced into zero-hours contracts or freelance status, that I'm sure my experience is quite common. Women go back to work, even when perhaps we're not quite ready. I'm glad there are films and TV shows, and books, where characters also reflect this reality, so we can at least have a way of talking about it, and not feeling alone.

Bergstein was very passionate about the Penny abortion storyline for these reasons. So passionate, in fact, that it very nearly sunk the whole thing. As she explains, when *Dirty Dancing* was made, the studio behind it did not have high hopes for it and expected it to go straight to VHS. And then suddenly, miraculously, they found a sponsor and a cinematic release looked possible. But only, the sponsor decreed, if the abortion storyline was removed. They didn't like it. They were concerned it would be controversial and off-putting to audiences. The company made skincare products and spot cream, and therefore wanted to appeal to the teenage market. Of course, teenage girls are probably the ones who need skincare products and realistic, non-judgemental depictions of abortion the most, but the CEO clearly couldn't see that.

Bergstein smiled sweetly, but didn't budge. The courage this took is quite astonishing when you think about it. *Dirty Dancing* was a labour of love for her. It was to prove her only real hit. Much of it was based on her actual life. It had taken every ounce of her energy and belief to get the thing made, and now, on the brink of success, she was willing to jeopardise all of it in order to save a political point she wanted to make. That access to legal and safe abortions was absolutely essential to the health and well-being of women. She had been smart too, in the writing of the film, and made sure Penny's abortion was so intrinsic to the plot that it could not simply be removed without the whole thing collapsing. And she had some advice for others:

What I always say to people – since people are always complaining that they put serious moral themes in their movies that get taken out – is that if you're putting in a political theme, you really better have it written into the story, because otherwise the day will come when they'll tell you to take it out. And if they can, it will go out. If it's in the corner of the frame, it will always go out.[5]

When *Dirty Dancing* came out, in 1987, 14 years had passed since Roe v. Wade made abortion legal across the United States. Bergstein has expressed surprise that people have become so secure about their relatively recent legal rights, and that she was even questioned as to why she felt it so necessary:

When I made the movie in 1987, about 1963, I put in the illegal abortion and everyone said, 'Why? There was Roe v. Wade – what are you doing this for?' I said, 'Well, I don't know that we will always have Roe v. Wade,' and I got a lot of pushback on that. Worse than that, there were also very young women then who didn't remember a time before Roe v. Wade, so for them I was like Susan B. Anthony, saying, 'Oh, just remember, remember, remember.'[6]

This was remarkably prophetic – as I write in 2019, with Donald Trump in the White House, and a swathe of conservative, evangelical politicians in roles where they are trying to dismantle these very rights, it all suddenly seems so fragile. Today, as I write this very line, the state of Texas is debating whether the death penalty should be applied to women who abort a foetus – yes, you read that right.

Bergstein is correct to say that we should not take anything for granted. And she was correct to stand her ground. It was still a huge risk at the time of release. Without the corporate sponsorship, the studio, Vestron, planned to give it a weekend in cinemas around America, and then shift it quickly to video release. But that never happened, because once women started to see *Dirty Dancing*, they told their friends to see it. And many saw it for the first time, and then went straight back to see it again. It became that most rare and wonderful thing: a success on its own terms.

Pro-choice campaigners have since called it the 'gold standard' in depicting an abortion on screen. They point to the fact that Penny is not judged by anyone, that she has her health as a priority, and is later told she will make a full recovery and have children in the future, if she wants them. The fault is not hers, rather the laws that drove her to seek out an illegal abortion in the first place. We do not have to watch the full procedure on screen, seeing her bleed and suffer. The bare minimum of her pain is required for us to get the idea, and it is upsetting to see, but our imagination does most of the work. It's a brief moment of sweaty, cramping horror, and then the next time we see her, she looks refreshed and relaxed, and optimistic about the future (well, who wouldn't be in that lovely dressing gown . . .)

I'm so glad this film came into my life when I was about to become a teenager. It is a touchingly responsible piece of work, that seems to care about the messages young girls pick up. Eleanor Bergstein once recalled a conversation with a cousin of hers, years later, in which the other woman said that she was only just realising the extent to which her moral and political views were influenced by the films she saw as a little girl. *Dirty Dancing* was almost certainly the very first depiction of an abortion I saw on screen in my life. Even if I didn't fully understand it the first few times, it must have shaped my opinions later. The information went in, and was processed without me even realising it.

Eleanor Bergstein's principled, careful way of weaving a difficult and upsetting issue into this film that is otherwise a joyful confection is now getting the applause it deserves. She has given many interviews around the subject, and journalists want to talk to her about it. Blog posts analysing *Dirty Dancing* as a feminist trailblazer of a film have popped up all over the internet. But there is still room for some confusion – I was amazed recently when talking to a room full of adults, all familiar with the film, at the number of people who said afterwards that they had either forgotten about the abortion, or hadn't even realised it was in there at the time. I think this is quite cool. She tucks it in to something light and entertaining. It's the ultimate case of 'show don't tell' – the advice given to most writers to avoid characters simply saying or reporting things they could be living and experiencing in the moment, in order to make the drama more interesting. People remember Penny, and they remember that she was a beautiful and talented dancer, before they remember she had a traumatic abortion. Her whole life is not just about the termination. I like that.

The point is, for Bergstein, abortion should not be a life-defining punishment or an ordeal. It is not a religious issue, and it should not be decided by religious beliefs. It should be decided by lawyers, not clerics or even politicians. Sometimes it is the best and most responsible course of action. This is what Bergstein believes, and I'm with her all the way.

Dirty Dancing showed me as a young girl, in the most delicate and gentle way possible, that should the problem arise in my life, I could count on other women to help me, just as Baby helps Penny, and the good men will back me up and support me through it. Penny is not alone – the touching gathering of all the other shocked dancers outside the cabin where she is moaning in pain also showed me that it doesn't have to be a source of shame either. You just have to ask for help, and a community will draw close. I loved Johnny for supporting Penny all the way. I loved Billy for doing his best to arrange the abortion itself. I loved Jake for treating Penny with such gentle respect. But most of all, I loved Baby for diving in there and making it happen, without a moment's hesitation. She gets the money. She learns the dance. She covers for Penny. She gets her dad. What a girl. What a woman.

Female solidarity and male support are the twin poles holding up *Dirty Dancing*. As Bergstein's cousin said, our attitudes are so influenced by what we watch when we are young, and I'm glad this was such a formative film for me. Even when I was a teenage Christian, and my church expected its congregation to be anti-abortion all the way, I equivocated. I kept my opinions to myself a lot of the time, but deep down, I knew what I really thought, and it wasn't what they thought.

And when I was having my own trouble with a failed pregnancy, I was so glad of the friends I did tell, who came to my house to cheer me up, my family who wrote me kind letters and held my hand, my husband who quietly backed me up on anything I said I needed, my agent's assistant who came to the hospital with me and sat next to me because I couldn't think who else I could bother while they were at work. I wish I'd told them more at the time, but contrary to some perceptions, I am not a big talker about my feelings.

I like to get on with things – the show must go on. Penny feels this too – she's spiky and sarcastic at first – 'Go back to your playpen, *Baby*,' she snaps, as our 17-year-old heroine fires out naive solutions to a problem she doesn't yet fully comprehend.

But later, Baby and Penny form a powerful alliance, and it's Baby who is the one allowed by the otherwise tough-as-nails Penny to see a moment of vulnerability. As she tucks Baby into her performance dress before Baby goes off to perform at the Sheldrake while Penny has the procedure, she breaks down quite suddenly. At first there's just a quiet 'thank you', barely heard. And then the tears come: 'I'm scared, Baby, I'm so scared.' Baby wraps her young arms around this complicated new friend and calmly replies, 'It'll be fine. You're gonna be fine.'

She very nearly isn't, of course, but sometimes that's all you need to get through it – another woman to confidently, optimistically, tell you you'll be fine, even if neither of you is quite sure. With the white-heat of Baby's burgeoning relationship with Johnny blinding us temporarily, it can be easy to miss this central female relationship of trust and compassion. But it's right there, if you know where to look. Thanks, *Dirty Dancing*. I owe you.

7
Will You Still Love Me Tomorrow?

I am on a train to Aylesbury. It is affectionately referred to as the Chiltern Turbo, and I have not been on one of these for around 20 years. It starts at Marylebone station and goes through my old home town of Amersham.

When we first moved there, this train did not exist, and commuters had to make do with the rather grotty old boneshakers that bother the Metropolitan Line (now rather more pleasant, it has to be said). Those greenbelt City workers who lived in the smarter Buckinghamshire towns and villages did not wish to be trammelled by such an uncomfortable service, though, and so a separate line was built that had nice hydraulic doors that hushed closed, little tables for your . . . I don't really know what for as take-away coffee was not a thing back then, but anyway, a nice touch. Somewhere to put your crisps. And, best of all, toilets.

The arrival of the Chiltern Turbo was extremely exciting – it went slow from Aylesbury to Amersham, through the posh stops, and then, luckily for me, fast from Amersham to Marylebone, meaning you could be in actual London – real, dirty, exciting London – in about half an hour, without ever having to encounter the existential despair that is Finchley Road station. Some of them stopped at Harrow-on-the-Hill, but if you closed your eyes, you'd never notice. This was amazing.

I am on my way to a performance of the live touring show of *Dirty Dancing*, at the Aylesbury Waterside Theatre. I have never seen this show before, and I have booked it now, in all honesty, as research for this very book. I knew of its existence, but in the same way I have also been aware of the existence of very life-like sex dolls, I have never felt compelled to seek it out. I prefer the real thing. But now, in the interests of professionalism (no, don't laugh), I am on my way to see it for the first time. I am quite excited, but also apprehensive.

I have tended to avoid 'the re-makes' of *Dirty Dancing* because I cannot believe I won't be disappointed. I have a hunch that the chemistry of the original casting will never be bettered, not in Aylesbury, not in London, not anywhere. The perfection of the moment, the bringing together of first-time director Emile Ardolino, a young choreographer Kenny Ortega and a relatively inexperienced writer in Eleanor Bergstein, with a cast hoping to establish themselves, and all that energy in one place makes a kind of alchemy – they were the pioneers, they were taking a chance that gold is in them there hills, and it was. And therefore probably not also to be found in a touring cash-in show. I think it somewhat smacks of cutting open the goose that laid the golden egg to get more, only to find no further eggs, and a dead goose on your hands. These things do not happen twice, and they are impossible to recreate. I have respect for the mysteries of natural chemistry and good casting, because they are rare.

But I remind myself to have some respect and a little faith – after all, Eleanor Bergstein actually wrote the live show herself, and who can blame her for wanting to mine a few more precious nuggets from her original creation? On the official *Dirty Dancing*: The Classic Story on Stage website, Bergstein's biography page says:

The multiple viewings by audiences all over the world made her suspect that what the audiences really wanted was to be more physically involved in the story. This would mean that its ultimate form should be one that combined dance and story and music onstage in a new way. It was also her chance to add new scenes not in the movie, as well as songs she had wanted for the movie and been unable to obtain.[7]

Hmmm, well, OK – I feel that *Dirty Dancing* has already achieved its 'ultimate form', and frankly, I don't like the sound of these 'new scenes', but I don't want to judge prematurely. The show is a huge success – it has been running for 15 years, is a certifiable box-office smash and had its share of excellent reviews when it opened, and so I tell myself I should stop being so snooty about it. It first opened in Australia in 2004, then in London in 2006, and has since been a commercial juggernaut, bringing joy to thousands of fans. Bergstein suffered and fought to get the film going in the first place, believing in herself when nobody else did, and so I begrudge her nothing. Enjoy your money, Eleanor! You deserve it . . .

And yet I feel a weird sense of gloom hanging over me. I try to attribute it to the fact that I am effectively riding back in time on this train, but perhaps it's also the cramped conditions. The mistake I have made is to unnecessarily travel at rush hour, so I got one of the last seats available on this packed commuter service out of the Big Smoke and into the countryside. I am a soft-handed, sleep-till-11, which meal are we meant to be on now? writer-type and I do not have the skills to basically sit on someone's lap for an hour and be fine with it.

But I get over it, and in a way, it's interesting to be amongst everyone on this train – my people, my middle-class, suburban, not-quite-the-country/not-quite-the-city people. I feel both immediately comfortable with the familiarity of it, but also slightly uneasy that nothing, absolutely nothing, has changed. It's as if I have boarded a 1995-shaped time warp. I swear to god, the woman across the aisle from me is wearing a coat I tried on in the Watford branch of Next when I was 15. The same slightly weary atmosphere that I remember is here, but also a sense that these people are pleased to be heading out of London, back to their nice quiet residential streets, with gardens front and back and a magnolia tree every half a mile or so. It's all about pints in old pubs with streams in the beer garden, a nice curry at the Indian with friends, and a barbecue on Sunday at the cricket club to look forward to. Nice lives. Nice, comfortable lives. Nothing wrong with that – it's something to aspire to.

The sliding view out the window is exactly the same, too. Loaves of terraced houses file away from the tracks, with huge Jurassic weeds growing up the backs of fences. Then we're at grey Harrow-on-the-Hill, where I bunked off work – not once, but twice – in order to see *Titanic* at the cinema on my own on consecutive afternoons. Then on through Hertfordshire, and I can recite the stations, though they are fewer on this line than the rumbling Metropolitan Line trains that clack alongside. Here's Chorleywood, where I went to school and church, and now we're on the short stretch to Amersham, which I took daily to get home from school for seven years of my life.

I crane my head awkwardly from my spot three seats from the window to see as much as I can, my brain gulping it all in. It's the same, all the same – the shop names, even the shop signs and awnings, all exactly the same. I feel both reassured and disappointed. Am I the same, then? Are the massive changes I think I have undergone since I left mere vanity on my part? I predict correctly that the train will empty at Amersham, and then continue into the greener, more exclusive, more expensive parts of Buckinghamshire with a more select clientele – ponies in paddocks, immaculate guest bathrooms, marble kitchen islands, you know what I mean. I am able to shift to a window seat now, and have an area of six seats all to myself. I smile the same smile I had when the same thing would happen as a teenager. Oh god, I haven't changed at all.

And now we're in Aylesbury, and I'm getting off the train and heading for the theatre. It's not far, and I see the hot pink glow of a lightbox with a poster in it, shining like a beacon to guide my path. It can only be for *Dirty Dancing*.

I join the steady stream of middle-aged white women heading into the foyer, and again feel pretty at ease, for I am also practically a middle-aged white woman, or at least not a million years off. There's no point pretending my natural habitat is a deep trance rave in a concrete bunker in Berlin, because it really, really isn't. A night out at a provincial theatre show is very much my safe place. Nothing can go wrong here. Look, there's even a Waitrose right next door where I can pop in to get a pre-show sandwich. I join the queue of other women, all also holding pre-show sandwiches, and nod and smile at one of them. We know where we're going. We know what we're here for.

Actually, there are a surprising number of middle-aged men here, I note, as I walk into the main entrance of the theatre and take a look around. Rather improbably, there is a group of bikers too, with beards, tattoos and chains, all sat round a bar table, drinking sparkling water and eating Pringles. Perhaps I have been too quick to judge.

I buy a programme and make the fatal mistake of noticing and approaching the merchandise stand. Reader, I bought everything. I got a pink tote bag, a Baby necklace, a Keep Calm and Carry a Watermelon water bottle, a Kellerman's Staff t-shirt, and a watermelon cushion. It came to £48.50. I am ashamed, but also exhilarated. I think it can only be the teenager in me, permanently broke, whispering, 'Buy it, buy it – you've got credit cards now, you can just buy it.' I blame her. I blame the discombobulating effect of an unexpectedly emotional train journey. I begin to wish I had gone to the Woking show instead, as this whole trip back in time is making my hormones overactive. It's not even that I want to buy this stuff because of the show, it's just that I am weak in the face of merchandise. So very weak.

I find my seat before I can spaff any more money I don't have on *Dirty Dancing* themed nonsense (the ticket alone has cost me £50 – 'It's all tax-deductable,' I mutter to myself, but I'm not sure it is. Where is the boundary for 'personal use' to be set? Is a watermelon cushion really a legitimate business expense? I just don't know anymore . . .)

The theatre is half empty. But that also means it is half full. There are quite a lot of older couples here, or small groups of women. The atmosphere is not quite feverish, more sort of post-daily dose of aspirin as recommended by the local GP. But it's nice, friendly and people smile and chat, and eat Maltesers, like I'm doing.

I wonder what people make of me, having basically swept the table at the merch stand, and now sitting here alone, in an otherwise empty row in the stalls, surrounded by my hot pink swag in what is clearly an expensive seat. 'Ah, one of those obsessive types we hear about, Mary – she's probably seen this several dozen times. Bless her. She probably thinks the cast are her friends, and they humour her by the stage door after the show.' I resist the urge to stand up and explain myself. Because frankly, I *am* one of those obsessive types about *Dirty Dancing*, it's just that until now I have been able to hide it by only watching the original film in private and mostly alone. Now I'm exposed, out in the open, and wearing a Baby necklace that is almost certain to give me a rash by the time I get home.

I so want to love this, but I'm feeling queasy. I almost feel like I'm cheating on someone. The lights dim, the curtain raises; it begins!

I am keeping an open mind. I am forcibly keeping it open because I hate it already. That girl is not Baby. She's very good, and her wig is excellent, but she's not Baby. They are not the Housemans. That's not Max Kellerman – no, DON'T leave a massive pause and play to the crowd when you say 'Ladies, if it wasn't for your father, I'd be standing here . . . DEAD,' and then wait for a laugh that never quite comes. No, don't do that – it's a throwaway line, it works best as a throwaway . . . and what's this now? This waiter, muttering to his mate after the Max Kellerman restaurant pep talk, 'It's the same in all these places – a bit of head in the woods maybe, but no conversation.' A bit of HEAD? It's ASS, a bit of ASS in the woods – at what point did someone decide alluding to a blow job is more acceptable to a regional theatre audience than merely grabbing a buttock? Is the actor just bored? Maybe it's the actor making up his own lines after already spending most of his adult life on tour with this show, and only those 23 words to keep him interested.

And oh god, we're about to meet Johnny. I feel a bit nervous. 'Bah-dah-dah-dah-dah-d-dah-BAH-DAH-BAH-DAH'

– the opening blast of that energising mambo, and here he is! And Penny. And they're TALL. Fucking hell, they're like giants. They're good dancers. They do all the right steps in the right order. But they're not Patrick and Cynthia, and that's not Jennifer Grey watching them. I can't do it. This feels all kinds of wrong.

I make it through the first half, despite the addition of an extra scene round a campfire, which begins with Lisa saying to Baby, 'Do you remember when there was the Bay of Pigs disaster with Cuba . . .' (I actually do involuntary snort at this) and ends with Tito saying to young Neil, 'I don't want you to go Freedom Riding with the bus boys down to Mississippi, kid – I know how it is down there, and you're like a son to me. I want you to come back in one piece.' I shake my head and tut quietly, and mercifully, the woman behind me catches my eye and I feel less alone – she gets it too. What's this scene for? Eleanor, I know you're proud of your political credentials, and the way many of these issues were cleverly laced into *Dirty Dancing*, but what the hell is this? No, no, no – no extra scenes, please. You cannot mess with perfection. Nothing more is required.

Later, I discover some of these scenes were in the original screenplay, and I send up a silent thank you to the editor who cut them out. A good editor is like gold dust. But clearly, Eleanor Bergstein felt they should go back in, and exercised her right to do so once she got her hands on a new production. I believe the editor was right . . .

As the show continues, I begin to wonder how this chemistry-less partnership between Fake Baby and Fake

Johnny is going to manage that crackling sex scene, but they just about pull it off. It's quite explicit actually, and unexpectedly sexy, but to be honest, that scene is so brilliantly structured and perfectly conceived that I defy anyone not to make it sexy. I could watch Little and Large do it, and still feel a bit of a fizz. It also rounds off the first half, with a gauzy curtain falling just as our couple reach their climax. A few men blink into the house lights as they come up, and one who is there on his own adjusts his trousers. I wonder if he comes here often.

I feel bad. I'm being negative, and it's entertaining, and well put together. It's slick, I'll give them that. And the cast are doing a great job – I don't want to criticise the performers. It's a tough job after a while, away from home for months, arriving in unknown towns, doing the show to a half-empty (sorry, half-FULL) room, then moving on to the next place. Missing birthdays, weddings, funerals along the way. There are going to be shows that feel a bit tired, a bit flat. It's a rainy Monday night in Aylesbury. No one is expecting theatre history to be made here tonight. It's not them, it's me. It's definitely me. I don't want anything else. I'm a *Dirty Dancing* purist – it's the original or nothing.

I stay in my seat as the gentle hum of contented interval chat vibrates around me. I don't want an ice cream. I don't know if I even want to stay for the second half. We are practically three-quarters of the way through the film's story and there's still an hour left of the live show. I wonder how they are going to fill the time. The word 'padding' springs to mind. And then there's the threat of more of those 'extra scenes' hanging over it all. One of the things I most admire about the film of *Dirty Dancing* is how tight it is. The plot rips along, and we're all done and dusted in just over 90 minutes. This, to me, is a triumph. When I watched it recently with my husband, I paused it at one point to see how much time Eleanor had taken to set up her story, characters, place and setting, and get us nicely headed into Act 2 – 37 minutes. She does a lot of storytelling in 37 minutes, and it's not clunky, it's just concise and well crafted. And at no point does anyone say, 'Do you remember when it was the Bay of Pigs disaster with Cuba?' Because it's not necessary. I don't want any of these extra scenes. I don't want any more of this. I decide to leave.

As I make my way out of the stalls, I pass a 70-year-old man who is leaning over a barrier and booming at an usher, 'I don't get it, I just don't get it,' as his embarrassed wife stands silently by, eating a vanilla ice cream. And I want to shout back, 'Watch the film! I implore you to watch the film! That's where the magic is, I promise.' But I don't. I just walk quietly out of the theatre, and back down the road to the station to catch the train to London, where I sit on an empty platform and text my husband that I have left early, but not to be sad, because I don't mind that I didn't like it. I wasn't expecting to. I hold my hot pink tote bag of presents for myself – souvenirs of something I never really went to – and wonder who to give them to.

I kept them all, of course. I love that Kellerman's t-shirt. The water bottle will come in handy. The Baby necklace is itchy, but sweet. The watermelon cushion was a mistake in retrospect, but I'm sure I'll find a use for it. And I'm being melodramatic, of course, but that feeling of needing to get out was real for a moment. I had anticipated it, but I didn't think I would actually abandon the whole show halfway through. I had even been offered a complimentary ticket when news of this book reached the theatre, but I decided to buy my own, so I would be free to write whatever I wanted. And it's not a bad show, not at all. I don't want to put anyone off going. The problem is that the original film is just so damn good, there's no point in trying to recreate it. And it makes me realise again how important and mysterious good casting is. There will never be another Patrick and Jennifer in those roles, and the chemistry between them cannot be manufactured. The film is bigger than the script and the songs and the choreography.

I also suspect that the half-empty (half-FULL) theatre tells us that perhaps the hardcore fans who initially turned out to see it when it began way back in 2004 have all seen it now, and those who are coming to Aylesbury on a Monday night are mostly doing so because, well, that's what's on, and it looks all right, and it's got some nice dancing in it, and pretty girls, and hunky men, and whoops! an abortion but let's not make a big deal out of it, and then there's the lift and we can go home – we only live 20 minutes away and there won't be any traffic by the time it's finished. I'm not sneering – that's me, that's my life. I will go and see *Starlight Express* at the Wycombe Swan any time you like. I love pantomimes, musicals and old school variety. I'll go to a Scout Gang Show in a church hall and enjoy it. But not this. Not for me. It was like a minor panic attack, or an allergic reaction. My heart beats for the one true *Dirty Dancing*, and there can be no others.

So, once again, it's only in the interest of research, and with one eye closed, that I now turn my attention to the 2017 film remake, starring Nicole Scherzinger. Here we go . . .

. . . OK, I'm back. Let's just say, I watched it so you don't have to. In the interests of professional integrity, I viewed it with pen and paper in hand. I made 12 pages of notes, but upon reviewing them, I see I have mostly just written 'no' over and over again. In fact, at one point, I have simply written, 'I do not have enough Nos for this. No.' It seems I was able to muster one more.

This thing is a bloated 2 hours 10 minutes long, adding a whopping half an hour to the original run time. Extra scenes have been added and, as with the stage show, they are totally surplus to requirement. What was subtly implied in the real *Dirty Dancing* is now revealed at every stage, with long monologues explaining every character's actions, behaviour and decisions. It's as if they were worried we missed it all the first time. We didn't. We understand nuance. This is all 'tell' and no 'show'.

I do not want to see Jake Houseman explain to Penny in unpleasantly controlling and judgemental tones that if she sleeps around she might get pregnant and this is a 'wake-up call'. The beauty and elegance of Jake's silence, his restraint and lack of judgement were some of the best things about Jerry Orbach's performance.

I don't want to see Marge Houseman asking for a divorce because she no longer gets enough action in the bedroom. The only good thing is that Penny simply says, 'I'm pregnant' to Baby, thereby no doubt clearing up much confusion for anyone under 15 watching this for the first time. But to those adolescents I simply say, 'YOU HAVE GOOGLE NOW. YOU CAN FIND OUT WHAT KNOCKED UP MEANS IN UNDER FIVE SECONDS. SO GO AND WATCH THE ORIGINAL ONE. THE REAL ONE. DON'T WASTE ANOTHER MOMENT OF YOUR PRECIOUS YOUTH ON THIS CHEMISTRY-LESS ABYSS.'

Fine, Abigail Breslin as Baby is a good actress, but she's a terrible and nervous dancer, even more terrible and nervous than the plot demands. Lisa (Sarah Hyland) is reduced to a simpering Manga cartoon, where once there was a rather brilliant undertow of knowing humour. And as for the 'framing device', where Baby goes to the Broadway show of her own life ten years later, and meets OLD JOHNNY, who is the choreographer of the show, and introduces him to her husband and daughter . . . and I can't go on, except to say to the producers, WHAT THE FUCK DO YOU THINK YOU'RE DOING? NO ONE WANTS TO SEE OLD JOHNNY AND OLD BABY STARING AT EACH OTHER WONDERING WHAT TO SAY BECAUSE NOW THEY'RE NOT SHAGGING ANYMORE THEY HAVE NOTHING IN COMMON.

OK, OK, I'm OK. I feel better now. Don't watch it. There's no need to do that to yourself. Just watch *Dirty Dancing* again. Please, take it from me.

I'm probably being a little bit childish, but there is a serious point here about the extent to which you can recreate magic. And also the desire to fiddle with things that are already perfect, simply to make a quick buck. It takes real imagination and courage to make something new, to take a risk on a bunch of people who have never really made a film before and allow them to see what they can do. This is part of the raw energy and passion that the original film exudes – you can't manufacture it. When you engage in a remake, you need a good reason. Yes, this version opens up the relationships a little more, but there are a million other shows that explore a middle-aged marriage and the problems that go with it better than this. I don't want to see Marge and Jake Houseman have make-up sex after discussing a separation. Make another original film about that, don't make the weak choice of trying to mitigate the risk by choosing something that has already been successful – it almost never works.

As I have said, one of things I have always greatly admired about Eleanor Bergstein's script for the real *Dirty Dancing* is how unbelievably tight it is. Not a word too many, not a pause too long. There's a lovely quick-quick-slow rhythm to the pacing that means you can race through set-up scenes and take your time where it matters. Padding it out with endless deep and meaningful looks and conversations only bogs things down – it's boring where it was exhilarating. One of the hardest things about being an artist, they say, is knowing when you're done. The temptation to add another brush stroke is huge, but the confidence is in standing back and saying, 'It's finished. It may not be perfect, but it's finished.' And then you have to give it away. *Dirty Dancing* was finished in 1987 and, luckily for us, it wasn't a one-off performance, it exists forever. Patrick Swayze and Jennifer Grey cannot be equalled, let alone bettered. The chemistry, the passion, the vulnerability – it's once in a million years, and every time someone tries to do it again, it only serves to remind us of that.

I'm not going to go on about it, and I don't want to pick apart every moment (OK, I do, but I'm not going to). Actors work hard, everyone on a film works hard, and it doesn't always turn out well. But here are three key scenes that I would like to briefly compare between the original film and the 2017 remake that I think illustrate my point:

'The Watermelon Scene' – AKA, Baby meets Johnny, dances with him, and feels sexually aroused for the first time in her life (apparently). In the real *Dirty Dancing*, or RDD as I shall call it, you can feel the heat coming off Baby and Johnny – they have chemistry immediately. She can't dance, but he teases it out of her until they are locked together for the briefest of moments, in symmetry. When he leaves her, she can barely stand up. For a few moments, they created their own world, a little Johnny and Baby bubble.

The intensity is there, and this is key to making everything that follows plausible. This sets everything up, and not a word is spoken. In fake *Dirty Dancing*, or FDD, none of this happens – partly because it is now a musical so Johnny is actually singing the song. This adds a kind of Kids from *Fame* element that strips it of all its gritty reality. And to make it worse, Penny bowls up behind them and steals Johnny away with a cat that got the cream smirk – no, this is just wrong. This is not a film about women competing for Johnny Castle's attention. This scene has one job, and one job only, and that is to show that – given half a chance – Johnny and Baby will have mind-blowing sex at some point. FDD is a dismal failure in this regard.

'The Money Handover Scene' – this is where Baby finds Johnny and Penny in the staff quarters to give Penny the money she has borrowed from her dad for the abortion. In RDD, Baby places the money in Penny's hand, and Penny gives it back. 'What?' says Johnny. 'Take the money, you should take the money.' I have always loved him for this. He knows the termination is the only way out for her and he is realistic about the world – this is some kind of miracle because they're not going to find the money any other way – and also supportive of her decision to have the procedure. He doesn't care about Baby at this point, he only cares about Penny, and here is a way out for her. Take it, he's saying, and we'll work out the issues later. But in FDD, it is Johnny who rejects the money, and hands it back to Baby, saying he is 'not a charity case'. No. No, no, no. That is not Johnny's decision to make, and to put it in his hands, and make it all about him, just makes him seem like a prick.

'The Father/Daughter Reckoning Scene' – this, for me, is the most heinous fuck up in FDD of all. In fact, I had to actually go back to the original script for *Dirty Dancing* to check I wasn't wrong about this, and I'm not. This is where Baby and her father have it out, where she tells him how she feels let down, and she's sorry she's a disappointment, but he is also a disappointment to her. In FDD, this is played not in a deserted autumnal gazebo, but next to a piano where Jake Houseman (who in this version is a some kind of frustrated song and dance man, earning the remake another 'NO' in my notes) has been singing to himself, wistfully dreaming of what could have been.

But the main problem is this: he does a lot of talking. Like, a LOT. And it sat wrong with me, and made me realise something about that scene in RDD that I have never consciously noticed before. And given that I may well have watched this film over 300 times in my life, that is something worth pointing out. In the original version of this scene, Jake Houseman says nothing. That's right, nothing. Not a single word. It was this I had to go back and check. Because that is bold writing, really interesting, brave, confident, assured writing. And the acting skill of Jerry Orbach to play such a memorable and much-loved scene without a single line is remarkable. As is Jennifer Grey's ability to pull off a monologue that feels like a conversation. She tells him what she's feeling, and he takes it, with tears in his eyes and nothing more. Beautiful, just beautiful. You fuck with that, you fuck with everything.

So, I'm done with remakes. I loaded up *Dirty Dancing Havana Nights* (the 2004 re-versioning set in Cuba in 1958) on my AppleTV box, but I'm not going near it now. I feel depressed at the very prospect. If you fall in love early, you fall in love hard, and I think I am a little bit in love with *Dirty Dancing*. Not just Johnny, but all of them. The whole thing. And watching someone else do it is like having an actor play an ex-boyfriend so you can recreate your first kiss – only a psychopath would do that. You cannot step in the same river twice, you cannot fake real laughter, you can't pretend to have fun.

Some things are just special, and your body is picking up on this unconsciously and sometimes you aren't even aware of why. For example, Jennifer Grey – who was not a trained dancer – has said that she was so frightened of doing the lift at the end of the film that she refused to rehearse it at all, and so the take we see in *Dirty Dancing* is her doing it for the first time. This is incredible. And it explains why it is iconic – the adrenaline, the build-up, it's all real. And then the response in the room from the other actors – all real. And this communicates itself, even through a camera lens, even 30 years down the line. We react to that on an instinctive level, and you can't make it happen again. The first take is often the best, and most good directors know it. It's why they always shoot the rehearsal.

Dirty Dancing is a one-off. It can't be made again, and it doesn't need to be. A sequel however, well . . . that's a different thing altogether. I'm so here for a sequel, and I wish they'd hurry up because Jennifer Grey isn't getting any younger despite what her plastic surgeon would have us believe. And I have an idea for one. Yes, I do. And I'm going to pitch it to you now. Ready? Here goes:

Katy Brand's Idea for a Dirty Dancing Sequel:

RETURN TO KELLERMAN'S
Baby (played by Jennifer Grey) is now 73 years old. She has a 56-year-old daughter (you do the maths – THAT'S RIGHT . . .!), and a 17-year-old granddaughter. On leaving Kellerman's in the summer of 1963, Baby started Mount Holyoke but

discovered she was pregnant. It can only have been Johnny Castle's baby. She kept the news from her parents, and went back to Kellerman's to find Johnny and tell him the news. But he is gone – the moment she left, Max Kellerman had told him to get out, and he had disappeared. She spent years trying to find him but couldn't, and ended up dropping out of college and raising her daughter alone. The shock of it gave her father a stroke and he never recovered. Her mother helped as much as she could. Baby shunned dancing and wouldn't have music in the house.

Her daughter grew up studious and bookish, and Baby married a professor willing to take her and a child on. They had a nice life, but it was devoid of spirit and passion. Her daughter never knew anything about Baby's wild summer in the Catskills. She married a boring man later in life, and had a child at 39. Baby dotes on her granddaughter, who brought some spontaneity and joy and back into her life.

As her granddaughter grew up, it was clear she had inherited an incredible natural skill and talent for dancing. Baby tries to deny it at first, but there are too many questions, and in the end, she confesses everything to her daughter and granddaughter. It's emotional, but they decide, the three of them, to go back to Kellerman's to see where it all began.

The resort is on its last legs – few guests, and no dancing lessons. It's tragic really. Neil Kellerman is still there, an old man, running things now, but he can't do much to change things. His grandfather predicted the decline and he was right. Baby walks in a dream from place to place, remembering that fateful summer. Patrick lives again in her memory (Mmm, Patrick.) She is sad.

But what's this? Her granddaughter seems to be firing up some interest with her amazing street dance routines, and decides to bring her troupe down to liven it all up a bit. Her mother is disapproving at first, but you can't suppress genetics – this is the progeny of Johnny Castle, after all. She is also quite into Neil Kellerman's son, who is a lot sexier than Neil Kellerman was, and is desperate to keep Kellerman's open for another generation.

Together, they livestream a street dance show so amazing that everyone wants to come and learn from Baby's granddaughter. And she and her mother move in there, and take over. Her mother hooks up with Neil Kellerman's son, and Baby moves into the old cabin where she and Johnny first got together, turning it into a beautiful chalet. Kellerman's is alive with dance once more, and the spirit of Johnny and Baby lives on.

END

I'd watch the fuck out of that, I truly would. And I'm a hypocrite too, because I'd be cashing in myself, although it's never cashing in when you're doing it, is it? No, no – it's an 'homage' when you're doing it. But at least it means we get another little dose of *Dirty Dancing* joy, and no one is an imposter, or an actor made to do a bad impression of something that cannot be bettered or, god forbid, tries to 'put their own stamp on it'.

Maybe one day someone will make a brilliant new version of *Dirty Dancing*, but it hasn't happened yet, and if not even the original creator can do it, I'm not holding out much hope for anyone else. This isn't to say Eleanor Bergstein won't give it a good try – she said in an interview with tabletmag. com in 2017 that for the first time she is interested in writing a sequel, 'which I never was before because I thought it could stand on its own.' Which it can. She won't be drawn on what happens between Baby and Johnny, but says enigmatically that she feels they 'have a future'.

What I'm saying is, I understand the urge to continue the success of something great. And to try to understand it, or even control it by stripping it down to its component parts and then building it up again, with a few extra bits and bobs to make it your own. But the point about a classic is that it will resist all that – a classic is perfect as it is. A classic cannot be remade. A classic is the superlative version of itself, and it holds a mystery and magic that guards against intruders. *Dirty Dancing* is just such a classic. Leave it well alone.

8
Overload

*A*ny success as large and resounding as that of *Dirty Dancing* brings with it a whole layer of super-fandom, where we devotees revel in every tiny detail we can uncover about the film, the cast, the production – anything. We want the gossip, we want the stories of what happened on set, how it was filmed, where it was filmed. And then we want to meet up on internet forums, and even in real life, so we can share in our obsession together. It becomes a whole industry in itself, and one that I am participating in and contributing to with this book. But I can't help it – I love it too much to stop now, so here is a chapter devoted to scratching that itch. For the real geeks and the true fans, amongst us.

First of all, I confess I love behind-the-scenes stories about films – I'll take any gossipy little story about 'what *really* went on' and enjoy every moment. I especially love stories about a big hit that nobody believed in at first; how it was very nearly scuppered before it even made it out into the world. What does it really take to make something great? Because it's never easy, and it hardly ever goes to plan. That is a great myth, and goes hand in hand with that wonderful Hollywood maxim, coined by writer William Goldman: 'No one knows anything.'

I thought of this, as did every other person with even a glancing professional connection with film, when David Cameron, then Prime Minister, said in 2012 that the British film industry should make more 'commercially successful films'. The irony was not lost on everyone in the industry that the most commercially successful film at the time Cameron made that remark was a French black and white silent film called *The Artist*, which also won every award going that year.

The point is, nobody could possibly have predicted that such a film would be the runaway hit of the moment, because if they could, they would all have been making silent black and white movies, which would have felt insane in 2012. And obviously, everyone is *trying* to make commercially successful films, but it's very hard to know what is going to hit. You have to make a wide variety of films and cross your fingers that one or two of them make enough money to cover the losses of the ones you got wrong, because . . . 'No one knows anything.'

It may be hard to believe, but there was a time when everyone involved with *Dirty Dancing*, with the possible exception of writer Eleanor Bergstein, thought it was an absolute stinker. According to an interview in the *Guardian* with Franke Previte, the co-writer of the Oscar-winning title song, '(I've Had) The Time of My Life', the mood had been initially low. After the song had won an Oscar, Previte met Patrick Swayze, who told him that they'd 'turned down 149 songs – our demo was the 150th'. According to Previte, Swayze said, 'To tell you the truth, we all hated the movie. We filmed the [final] dance scene first, but we didn't have a song then. So we were like, "Let's just get this piece of shit over with."' In fact, Previte goes on to say that the song transformed the filming process, which had been initially glum and pessimistic. Apparently, once the cast heard it, they wanted to go back and reshoot scenes with it playing in the background as it brought a 'vibe' to the set that had been previously lacking.

Dirty Dancing started life on the cutting room floor. Eleanor Bergstein describes how she wrote an erotic dance scene for another film, *It's My Turn*, which was later edited out. Despite this early rejection, the scene stayed with her – the power of it, and the intensity. She felt she could build on that to make a whole story, and so *Dirty Dancing* was born. This is a perfect attitude to take – even though she experienced that initial rejection, she didn't give up. She felt instinctively that what she had written was good and had value, even if others disagreed. I imagine that it is this drive and belief that got her film made. Because without that, it wasn't going to happen.

A piece in the *New York Times* in 1997 by Ann Kolson explained what happened:

It was over lunch with Ms. Bergstein in a restaurant on the Upper West Side of Manhattan in early 1985 that Linda Gottlieb, then a producer for MGM, first heard the term 'Dirty Dancing'. 'Eleanor, that's a

*million-dollar title!' Ms Gottlieb remembers exclaiming.
MGM financed development of the movie, but when the
studio changed management, it dropped the project. Ms.
Gottlieb began soliciting studios. 'I was turned down by
everyone who could say no,' she said. 'I kept hearing the
same responses: it's small and it's soft.'*[8]

Linda Gottlieb became the producer of *Dirty Dancing*, and
set about trying to raise money elsewhere. She clearly believed
in the project and was willing to push to find the right team.
And ultimately, she did, although it didn't always run entirely
smoothly – people had to be convinced. For example, when
Eleanor Bergstein and choreographer Kenny Ortega went to
meet prospective director Emile Ardolino, they showed him the
dancing they intended to build the film around. At dinner, Eleanor
got up, grabbed Ortega, and spontaneously began an improvised
and quite erotic routine. According to the *New York Times*,
Ardolino was so embarrassed he left the room. But it obviously
made quite an impression on him, because he later said of the
famous 'staff dance party' scene, 'I really wanted the audience
to feel what it was like for Baby to be in that room. It's exciting,
it's sexually charged, and I certainly wanted that on the screen.'

It starts with the dance and the seduction, and the rest
follows. I love this fact, because that danced seduction scene
between Baby and Johnny is the very heart of the film. Baby is
the one who makes it happen, but Johnny can't resist the force
of her will; when they start dancing together, they discover
that despite their many differences they are simply meant to
be. It's all in that one scene – it is *Dirty Dancing* in a nutshell.

Bergstein has been keen in recent years to highlight the political aspects of the film, and sometimes has even suggested that this was the whole reason for its inception. I'm sorry but I don't quite buy that. I don't mean to be disrespectful to the writer of one of the greatest films of all time, but I think she does herself a disservice. I don't think she even quite knew what she'd written at the time, but I'm pretty sure she didn't intend it originally as a manifesto with a bit of a love story thrown in. I'd actually be kind of sad if she had. I don't think, as some others have said, that *Dirty Dancing* was simply a vehicle for campaigning for abortion rights for women, disguised as a romantic drama. Nor do I think it started life as a feminist piece about empowerment, or equality. It may have become those things, and all these strands are absolutely present in it, but primarily, it is a great (and rare) story about a young girl coming of age, and learning how to be a woman through the joy and power of dance. Which, frankly, is still a political statement in itself.

Eleanor Bergstein's early interviews stress this far more than the political aspects: and she has said it is partly autobiographical, because she had experienced all that Baby experiences in *Dirty Dancing* first-hand – she was from a Jewish family, the daughter of a doctor, who spent summers with her family in Catskills resorts, where she learned to dance with the hotel staff as a teenager. She even has a sister called Frances. It's popular entertainment with a real message, and that's enough for me – I don't think anyone should be nervous of describing it as such. It doesn't make it trivial or frivolous, and attempting to recast it as a heavyweight piece of political drama actually undoes some of its appeal.

And Bergstein has done something very unique and clever with the story's structure. The two basic romantic storylines are: 1) man and woman meet, dislike each other, but then over time and as they reveal their true selves, realise they are in love, and 2) man and woman meet, it's love at first sight, but they are then cruelly separated, working their way back to each other against all odds. Most of the great love stories will be a version of one of these two basic stories, from Beatrice and Benedict in *Much Ado About Nothing* (type 1) to *Romeo and Juliet* (type 2). It has often been pointed out that the reason everybody loves *Pride and Prejudice*, and why it's so frequently voted the best book of all time, is that Jane Austen cleverly weaves both these storylines through the novel at once – Elizabeth Bennet and Mr Darcy are type 1, and Jane and Mr Bingley are type 2. But in *Dirty Dancing*, we have a type 1 storyline that shifts to a type 2 halfway through, with the same couple. How intoxicating.

Throughout the history of telling stories, class, family or tribe has been used as the device to keep the lovers apart, and Johnny and Baby are no different. And then something will come along that transcends these petty squabbles, and makes everyone realise we're really just the same – it can be a death, or some other crisis. But in *Dirty Dancing* it's a positive force – it's the dancing. And it's sex and love. Dancing, sex and love – this holy trinity will save us all.

So, with a great script in place, they now needed money. As all the major studios had said no, Gottlieb had to fundraise elsewhere. Eventually, a small company who mainly focused on making straight-to-video films, Vestron, agreed to provide the cash. It was half what was originally budgeted, but the team could see it was their only chance, so they slashed costs wherever they could, and finally, production could start. The casting was complicated. At one stage Val Kilmer was lined up to play Johnny Castle, and Sarah Jessica Parker (a former dancer) and Sharon Stone (Sharon Stone!) both auditioned to play Baby. Val Kilmer turned it down and so Billy Zane was cast instead, but he was removed from the role because of a lack of chemistry with Jennifer Grey, who had by now finally been confirmed. Her audition tape, available to watch online, shows that only she could have done the job. It's nervy but warm, straight-talking but also innocent. She is simply charming and sexy in a way that seems natural but not quite fully under control. She is girlish but strong. She's Baby.

And here comes Patrick Swayze, the only man for the job – in fact, Bergstein had wanted him all along. As journalist Hadley Freeman says in her book, *Life Moves Pretty Fast: The Lessons We Learned from Eighties Movies*, 'No one other than Swayze, the son of a cowboy and a ballet dancer, could have captured Johnny's feminized masculinity.' This is so true it hurts – he has a delicate grace and vulnerability, while also being 100 per cent alpha, something that very few men can pull off. He is also not sleazy, which is also absolutely key, as a Billy Zane or a Val Kilmer – who both have a slightly cruel twist to the mouth – may have made the whole relationship seem like an exploitation. When Johnny says, 'They were using me!' to show Baby how he has been taken advantage of by the older women at Kellerman's, Swayze manages to make this sound plausible, even heartbreaking. He's just so damn sincere in everything he does. He can't lie – you can see what he's thinking and feeling all the time. Johnny is never a threat, he never seems predatory – without this quality, the whole thing would sink.

The filming itself didn't go very smoothly. It is fairly well known now that even though Jennifer Grey and Patrick Swayze were individually perfect for their respective roles, they did not always get along during the filming. During the audition process, they did what's called in the business a 'chemistry read' – a meeting of the two leads before casting is finalised to make sure there is a genuine attraction that will come across on screen – which went very well, but this was soon lost in the stress and strain of making a film that everyone thought was going to fail.

So the budget was small – only $4 million – and a small budget always means an uncomfortable shoot. 'Let's see the money on screen,' the producers like to say, and although everyone always agrees with this in principle, they also know it's going to mean long days and no luxuries.

For example, 'rain cover' on a shoot is a luxury – it means you can move scenes inside if a storm is coming, but this relies on keeping multiple locations available, even on days where you are not scheduled to be there, and this is expensive. It also means having members of the cast at your disposal at all times, so you can change the shooting schedule at a moment's notice. This is not an option open to a project with limited cash, where every dollar is accounted for just to get the thing made at all. Apparently, it rained almost all the time during the shoot, though they have done a good job masking it. I wonder if Lisa's line, 'I'm so sick of all this rain', as she is cooped up in the cabin with her family for another day, was added to try to acknowledge the terrible weather. Or maybe she simply improvised it!

But there was nothing they could do about it, except press on and try to stay on schedule. Hence the reason the lift in the lake scene was shot in weather so freezing Jennifer Grey's nipples got their own agent after release, and there are no close-ups due to blue lips and shivering. Apparently, the inspiration for the whole scene was dance legend Gene Kelly, who recommended learning lifts this way to his protégé, *Dirty Dancing* choreographer Kenny Ortega. The story goes that Ortega even joined the actors in the icy lake to help them get it right. Or perhaps he just felt bad . . .

The reason it was cheaper to film in the cold autumn, rather than shoot in the high season of summer, was the price of the hotel locations, who would have charged a premium to shut down in the lucrative warmer months. Most of the location shoots take place at a hotel called Mountain Lake Lodge in Virginia and a resort called Lake Lure in North Carolina. To make the exteriors feel summery, they had to spray the leaves on the trees with green paint, and put green food dye into the grass. It rained a lot, and I can only imagine the mess as all that colour started to drip and run.

The discomforts that come from shooting on a tight

budget often seem small at first, but can compound and build over time, becoming the sort of thing that can test the most amicable of professional relationships, and tested it was. The scene where Jennifer collapses in giggles repeatedly as Swayze runs his hand down the inside of her arm, as his expression becomes more and more irritated, was real – she was really ticklish; he was really pissed off. Swayze said in his autobiography, *The Time of My Life*, about working with Grey, 'She seemed particularly emotional, sometimes bursting into tears if someone criticised her. Other times, she slipped into silly moods, forcing us to do scenes over and over again when she'd start laughing.'

In fact, the relationship broke down to such an extent that the two stars had to be shown their original chemistry read audition tape to remind them that they had once enjoyed working together, or even being in the same room. It seemed to work, as the 'Lover Boy' scene, where they playfully mime the lyrics to the song 'Love is Strange' by Mickey & Sylvia as they work through some dance moves was apparently only an improvised warm up, during which the director wisely and brilliantly instructed the cameras to roll on. And I'm so glad he did, because it's a great moment in the film, and in the evolution of Baby and Johnny's relationship – relaxed and light, where so much of it is intense and worried.

People who haven't had to hang around a film or TV set often think filming is glamorous, but usually it isn't, and on a long shoot where there isn't much money to go around any creature comforts get abandoned quickly. For the first series of my TV sketch show, *Katy Brand's Big Ass Show*, we didn't want to spend money on dressing rooms and trailers, so I got changed in the producer's car. I was doing three of four complete costume changes most days to get through the characters we needed, and I remember contorting myself in the back seat, trying to get all manner of ludicrous outfits on and off, with bits of A4 paper stuck to the windows for some privacy. In fact, more than once I thought of Baby changing in the back seat of Johnny's car after the dance at the Sheldrake and this felt quite similar, except that there was no one in the car with me, and I was going from a Kate Winslet costume (covered in mud, to be 'normal') to a Kate Moss costume (15-year-old school disco bitch).

During the course of my acting life, I have been bitten by insects all over my body while repeatedly running through a forest in a leotard; I've spent a whole afternoon stood up to my waist in a filthy pond; I've sat on a busy roundabout in a ripped pink ballgown while being filmed from afar so none of the drivers knew what I was doing and yelled at me for the whole two hours, and I've been made to lie in a wet and muddy ditch with my face in the dirt for several hours. I've lost track of the times I've had to film in pouring, freezing rain dressed for a summer's day because we simply didn't have the money to change the schedule. And to add insult to injury, the whole crew are right in front of you dressed in warm coats and huddled under umbrellas. Rain doesn't show up on camera, you see, so you can often continue as if it's not there. In fact, when you do see rain on camera, it is usually fake. For example, the very visible rain in Gene Kelly's famous *Singin' in the Rain* dance sequence was made by mixing water with dried milk powder so it would be seen on film. I cannot imagine the smell in the studio after a few hours of that stuff falling! Like an abandoned dairy farm, or an old fridge.

Many of the scenarios I have described above were entirely my fault, since I wrote the shows. The advantage to this is that I wrote the scenes because I thought they'd look funny on screen, and so I kept that in mind while out in lashing rain, dressed completely inappropriately. But it can get to you a little bit after a while, and make you behave differently than you normally would. Many's the time I have been picked up before 5am, driven to a location to have make-up done for two hours, then filmed constantly for 12 hours, before driving home to learn another ten pages of script. And then getting up to do it all again the next day.

After 8 solid weeks of this, you do feel you would like it to stop. But then you get to the end and hug everyone, laugh and cry a bit, have a little rest, a nice hot bath, a glass of wine, imagine how crap and miserable you'd be doing anything else, and gear up for the next job. It's amazing how selective your memory can be when it wants to block out unpleasant experiences (I think this can be the only explanation for women choosing to give birth more than once . . .).

I'm not so much complaining (I hope) as explaining why tempers get a little short sometimes on set, and things get blown out of proportion. You're often away from home for long periods, and too tired to talk to anyone you love on the phone in the evening, and so you can end up feeling isolated and irritable. You take it out a little bit on your equally irritable co-star, and suddenly you're both glaring at each other with your arms folded when you're supposed to be pretending to make mad passionate love for the first time. You want to be huddled up in a dressing gown with a cup of tea, rather than take all your clothes off in front of 40 people you barely know in a cold room. It takes a skilled and diplomatic producer and a sensitive director to work out what to do in these situations, and it seems *Dirty Dancing* was blessed with both in the forms of Linda Gottlieb and Emile Ardolino. They must have been sweet-talking geniuses, or we wouldn't have anything like the sizzle we see on screen. And to be honest, the tension probably contributed a little to that too. You never know where the breaks are going to come, so be wise and turn anything to your advantage.

It's also a very intense environment – it becomes your whole life. You get a call sheet every night that tells everyone what is happening the next day. The sheet also tells you what time you will be picked up to go to the set, what time breakfast, lunch and dinner is, and what time you will finish. Food is provided by a catering truck with limited choices, so you get used to getting what you're given and liking it. If you want to go to the toilet during filming, you have to ask permission in front of everyone, and usually a runner will accompany you and stand outside the cubicle while you do your business, and then walk you back to the set. This is so you don't get lost, or make a run for it (when it's really going badly), as the one person they really can't do anything without is the actor. Everyone else can ultimately be replaced with varying degrees of simplicity, but the face on-screen is indispensable once you have started and got a good chunk of it in the can.

What I'm saying is, it comes as no surprise to me, or any other actor, that Jennifer Grey and Patrick Swayze had a few points of tension during the filming of *Dirty Dancing*. If there's more money in the budget, it's easier – the shoot days are less intense as you don't have to cover as many pages, you can have bigger trailers for more privacy, you can switch to interiors if the weather is bad. It doesn't mean they hated each other, and truly that final scene, that was reshot when they got the music, could not have been achieved if there was some permanent dislike. And at least there was a little bit of fire in their bellies when they really had to shout at each other, and perhaps it was necessary to bring that chemistry to life on screen. We have all responded to it, and it's that little pinch of spice that takes a film from good to great. In fact, I have often done the best work of my life during times when I thought I may spontaneously combust with the pressure and stress of it all. When life's too comfortable, the work can suffer because the urgency goes out of it. I think anyone who has engaged in anything creative or challenging will probably agree. If you don't really need the work, the passion can die, and you're more likely to give up and not bother.

There were other issues to contend with on the *Dirty Dancing* shoot – for example, the actress who originally played Marge Houseman, Lynne Lipton, shot the opening scenes, and then became very ill after falling into the lake at the hotel location. The schedule was tight, with only 44 days to complete everything they needed to, and she simply wasn't well enough to come back in time. So Kelly Bishop, who had been cast as Vivian the Bungalow Bunny, was suddenly switched into the role following a personal recommendation from Jerry Orbach, who played Jake Houseman. Lynne Lipton was platinum blonde, but Bishop has flaming red hair. If you look closely in the opening scene as the Housemans drive up to Kellerman's you will see Marge is blonde. But when they arrive, and she gets out of the car to be greeted by Max Kellerman, her hair is that distinctive red. This also meant that the amazing Miranda Garrison stepped up to play Vivian, and I'm so glad she did, because something about her melancholy and faded glamour did the job perfectly.

Further trouble was ahead, with the set being broken into and damaged during filming, and a mass outbreak of food poisoning, but somehow they all got through it. They had to! And joy of joys, Eleanor Bergstein herself can briefly be spotted dancing behind Patrick Swayze in the scene where Baby comes to get him to rescue Penny, so at least some perks came with the responsibility of firefighting and making it all happen.

Once the filming and editing was completed, the battles continued. Vestron, the small studio that stumped up the money after all the major studios had rejected it, still didn't know they had dynamite on their hands ('No one knows anything . . .') and planned one weekend on limited release in a handful of cinemas, before taking it straight to VHS. They thought they would make money in the long term, through rentals and sales, and networks picking it up to broadcast in tricky-to-fill late-night slots. The limited initial outlay could be made back over time – many deals are done with this in mind. Then a sponsor stepped in, an acne cream (some say it was Clearasil though that has not been 100 per cent confirmed – I imagine they'd want to keep quiet about it . . .), who saw a teen market in the making and wanted to exploit the connection. After they saw the final edit, clocked the abortion storyline, and accepted that Eleanor Bergstein was not going to cut it out, they withdrew funding.

In a way, it is probably the low budget that saved the film in the end. It is known in creative work that – almost always – the more money you receive for your work, the more control you are forced to give away. Modern movie moguls usually remove all final edit rights for just this sort of reason, and in a different time and a different circumstance, it's likely that Bergstein would not have had the power to make the decision to reject the sponsorship and keep the abortion storyline. Someone else, someone more compliant, would have been brought in to make the necessary cuts, with maybe a couple of reshoots to join up the story, and the sponsorship would have been in the bag. When directors or writers get tearful at awards and thank the producers for 'fighting for this little movie' it is easy to dismiss them as being over-emotional luvvies, but often it means that the producer was willing to forgo some more money from a large corporation to keep the original creative vision intact. It's worth thanking them for, even if you do get a bit tearful on stage, or even reach the heights of full-blown, snotty hysteria. The million fights that are fought, won, and lost behind the scenes can make or break a film.

In that first weekend, following the film's release on Friday 21 August 1987, *Dirty Dancing* proved to be a hit, and so the cinematic released was extended and extended. And it wasn't just teens who were going to see it, it was grown women, who were telling their friends, and then going again a second or third time. The film smashed all expectations.

Since its release, *Dirty Dancing* has made over $200 million. It is one of the best-loved films of all time, spawning remakes, merchandise, tribute acts; inspiring first dances at weddings, proposals, and perhaps even infidelities. Every decision, from small to big, and even ones that will have seemed disastrous at the time – the casting of relatively unknown actors, the halving of the budget, the filming in a rainy autumn, the shock of losing funding due to refusing to cut the abortion story – has contributed in some way to its success, and Eleanor Bergstein's dogged determination to have her film made and put out, her way, is an inspiration.

The soundtrack too is an absolute triumph, and many people talk of it in awed tones as much as they do the film itself. Eleanor Bergstein brought in many of her favourite records, and she personally oversaw the track list. During her first meeting with director Emile Ardolino and choreographer Kenny Ortega, the deal was sealed when she turned up with a bag of .45s and played them, while dancing herself. The two original songs '(I've Had) The Time of My Life' and 'She's Like the Wind' (written and performed by Patrick Swayze) went on to be huge hits, with the signature track winning an Oscar for Best Song.

When the soundtrack was released in 1987, it went straight to number one, beating Michael Jackson's *Bad*, and has since sold 35 million copies. A second soundtrack was released, which has also sold nearly 10 million copies, even though it features the lesser-known Latin dance tracks. It seemed anything to do with the film was gold, defying all the early issues and negativity.

So, what's become of the dream team that put everything on the line to make a masterpiece? What's Eleanor Bergstein up to now? Well, she continues to write and, as I've said before, she conceived and wrote the live show that still plays around the world. She is finally getting the credit she deserves for what has in the past been criminally undervalued and dismissed. So much art made by women, for women, over the past 100 years or so is now thankfully getting a second look, and *Dirty Dancing*, which was rejected by all the male executives at all the major studios, and then sneered at by all the most senior male film critics on its release, is one such work. Bergstein has been revelling in the moment, it seems, and giving generous interviews whenever she is asked. It is great to see.

Other members of the team have not fared so well. Patrick Swayze went on to work on some major blockbusters, including *Ghost* and *Point Break*, but his life force was tragically cut short when he died in 2009 of pneumonia and pancreatic cancer. He was a sensitive and complicated man, spent some time in rehab for his alcoholism, smoked 60 cigarettes a day, and briefly retired from show business to breed horses. He was married for life to a woman he met when they were both teenagers, when she started taking dance classes with his ballet teacher mother. How poetic is that? He was born to play Johnny – it must have seemed like his own life from time to time.

Jennifer Grey has sadly made her face into a whole other person since filming *Dirty Dancing*. She was already a little bit famous from her role as Ferris Bueller's sister in the cult hit *Ferris Bueller's Day Off*, and she was steeped in the entertainment world as the daughter of Joel Grey, the dancer who played the MC in *Cabaret*, starring Liza Minnelli. But Baby was her part, and she has suffered perhaps from just being too good at it. She is Baby for all of us, and because we all identify so strongly with her, we don't really want to see her playing anyone else. Perhaps this is why she has to turn into someone else with the help of a plastic surgeon, though she has said she now regrets it. She has had some success, appearing in *Friends* and as a judge on *Dancing with the Stars* (the US version of *Strictly Come Dancing*), but you have to feel for her – a part as huge as Baby isn't always great for an actor's career. But the fact is she created an icon, a role model for teenage girls everywhere. 'Baby' will outlive her, and me, and hopefully inspire generations to come. She's got to be happy with that – I hope she is.

Jane Brucker who played Lisa Houseman continues to act, but her comedy skills have not really been called upon since *Dirty Dancing*, in which she gives a subtly hilarious performance. She co-wrote the nonsensical 'Hula Hana' song she sings in the talent show, so she will always have that to be proud of. We still don't know what the song means, but it is very, very funny.

Jerry Orbach (Jake Houseman) was already well established on Broadway, and also appeared in Woody Allen's excellent *Crimes and Misdemeanors*. He was famously in *Law & Order* until his death in 2004. He was a member of the American Theater Hall of Fame, and even has part of a New York street named after him.

Cynthia Rhodes has to take a bow for being in three of the most iconic dance films of the 1980s, and possibly of all time – *Flashdance*, *Staying Alive* and of course, *Dirty Dancing* as Penny Johnson. She retired from showbiz at the beginning of the 1990s when she met and married singer Richard Marx and had three kids. This seems a wise move, as she is the embodiment of the 1980s American dream woman, and it was very dignified of her to see that, and leave her best work in that decade.

But the prize for most unexpected and chequered post-*Dirty Dancing* life has to go to Max Cantor, who played sleazy Robbie Gould. I am simply going to quote Hadley Freeman again, and give her the credit for turning up this nugget because there is no good reason not to. OK, here goes – brace yourself:

> *Max Cantor had probably the creepiest post-eighties teen movie career of anyone. After a privileged New York upbringing and a very brief acting career he became an investigative journalist. He came across a story about a cannibalistic cult in downtown New York and, in order to gain their trust and get the story, he started taking drugs. He soon became addicted and was eventually found dead. Some alleged he was killed by the cannibal Daniel Rakowitz, but others say he simply overdosed. Whatever the truth, it's hard not to think poor old Robbie should have stuck with Ayn Rand and stayed away from the cannibals.[9]*

Jesus. What to say to that? I guess in the end, he really did go slumming.

A monster hit like *Dirty Dancing* inevitably changes actors' lives. It can be a mixed blessing to be in something like it, but I'm not going to feel too sad, because I can watch it any time I like. And I do. And when I asked around, I found I am very much not alone. It has inspired many, many fansites, blogs, articles, and groups. There are regular feature screenings around the world, where people come dressed as their favourite characters and sing and dance along. One such event, Secret Cinema, which reworks cult hits for an audience of fans who come along in costume and act out parts of the film, hosted a special event for *Dirty Dancing* in 2016, which was described by the *Guardian* as 'the UK's biggest hen party'. In her review, Kate Hutchinson sets the scene:

> For summer, the blockbustering site-specific behemoth has recreated randy coming-of-age classic Dirty Dancing. As usual, at a secret London location, there are interactive re-enactments and festivalesque frippery foreshadowing the film itself, elevating it from 'outdoor screening in a field' to what fancy folk call 'experiential cinema'.[10]

That night, I was performing a preview for my live comedy Edinburgh show, 'I Was a Teenage Christian', for ten people in a London pub, and therefore could not attend. In retrospect, I should have simply ditched the preview, grabbed a watermelon and headed on over to Secret Cinema. My show turned out to be good in the end, but I think that particular preview is best forgotten.

To get over my heartbreak at not going to the biggest *Dirty Dancing* cosplay event of all time, I asked someone who was there, Vix Leyton, a PR expert and burgeoning stand-up comedian, what it was like:

> The Dirty Dancing Secret Cinema was a perfect experience as a long-term fan of the film. The love for the film was evident in the attendees, from the absolute attention to detail in getting the costumes just right to the amount of watermelons being carried, and it truly was like stepping into Kellerman's. The dance floor was full

of sparkly-eyed fangirls, but we were infiltrated by pro-
fessional dancers, who were randomly picking 'guests'
to go for a whirl – this was enough to make me sick
with excitement all by itself, but being jostled out of the
way by a girl carrying watermelons was probably one
of my favourite moments of my whole life. What fol-
lowed was a faithful replay of the film, in real life, from
Johnny and Penny arriving, to him sweeping Baby up. It
was such a lovely, communal feeling of joy – seeing that
dancing up close was another level, and you could see
everyone mouthing along and subconsciously replicating
the moves that we all learnt in our bedrooms years and
years ago. It was a perfect summer night.

I mean, could you ask for a better time? And this feeling of
being part of a community is real. From the accounts of the
popularity of the Secret Cinema, it was clear that this was
a film that meant a huge amount to a lot of people. Having
nurtured my love alone for so long, I was now becoming
increasingly and joyfully aware of all my fellow obsessives out
there. I wanted more direct contact, and thanks to technology
and social media, it was easy to find. For the purposes of this
very book, I asked on Twitter what people most loved about
Dirty Dancing, expecting a couple of dozen replies. Hundreds
of answers poured in, and I read every single one, feeling a
warm glow grow inside. Some of my favourite replies were:

@SarahEHBurr Through our teen years, my best friend

and I used to take turns in being 'Baby' when we watched it together so we could be in the centre of the narrative.

@keynko Gappy memories of a warm summer evening with my bestie @wobblymouse We went to the cinema to see it when it was released. We danced down the street singing, full of hope for future full of love & romance. I think of her whenever I see it. In fact I will have to watch it today!

@manchester10uk Every Wednesday my mum doing her ironing watching it for the millionth time.

@LizzyLoly That sweet and innocent girl quickly growing up and becoming more worldly, but still being led by values and a sense of what's right – very empowering!

@ETimsnet The most upbeat feelgood film about backstreet abortion ever.

@studyinpink1 It showed the teenage me that it was OK to be different, that you didn't have to be the conventional, pretty and pliant one; as long as you were true to yourself even the hottest guy in the room would love you. Still a stone cold classic.

@JMBrand [my sister!]It was the first time I saw adults, who weren't parents, living cool lives.

@chuckiestealady so many things (esp Mr Swayze through the female gaze) but mostly seeing an unmarried woman (Penny obv) get a guilt-free abortion and happily recover is seriously liberating and horrifically rare in a film.

@runningguern I still use the phrase 'I'm doing all this to save your ass, when all I want to do is drop you on it' as an under-the-breath mantra at work.

@stafford_ross DD will always remind me of my wife who passed away last year as she loved this film.

It's hard not to feel a lump in your throat at that last one, and I'm glad he has something special to remember her by.

This was a fraction of what was sent, and they kept coming. It made me think about my favourite moments, some of which I realised were a little weird – I always liked Billy's goofy surprise and pride in the staff dance party, where he says of Baby, 'She came with me, she's with me!' It set up a sweetness and an innocence to the whole thing that helps move us to the sudden sexuality of that first dance in that hot, hot room.

I like Baby self-consciously pulling the wig off her head when Johnny walks up to Penny in the wig show by the lake, and ruffling her hair to try to look sultry for him while he barely notices – been there, my friend. The pleasure Baby takes in Johnny's body when she seduces him, and the way he screws up her top before he tosses it away – OMFG. Does it get any better than that?

The catch in Baby's voice when she calls out 'Johnny' to stop him walking away from her when they have been busted by Penny, making a noise like a tiny little bird about to fall out of its nest. I met a man called Johnny, and though we shared a kiss, it could never have worked because I just kept doing impressions of this moment and it drove him mad. It was also not at all sexy.

And the two comic moments provided by two secondary female characters in the closing minutes of the film. 'I think she gets this from me' is perfectly delivered by Kelly Bishop as Marge Houseman, and marks the only moment of real spark for her character. And of course the brilliant Jane Brucker performing her own composition, the incomprehensible 'Hula Hana', and that slow-motion kneel and kowtow that always made me laugh, and still does. Of course, I love all the big moments too, but these little bits are the hooks I also look forward to when I watch it again. They will be different for everybody.

One of my geekiest moments came early in my *Dirty Dancing* obsession. During my hundreds of repeat viewings, I became so familiar with what I was supposed to be looking at in a scene that I started to scan the TV screen, looking into the backgrounds, watching the extras, finding little errors. I feverishly studied it all to the point where I noticed the top of Baby's knickers as she lies back in bed SUPPOSEDLY NAKED. I called a summit of my closest friends to reveal this news, and lined up the video to the exact point in the film, paused it, and pointed in triumph at the clear line of elastic and lace that was meant to be cleverly covered by the duvet but WASN'T. This was a CONTINUITY FAIL, and I knew I was becoming more mature when I was old enough to be willing to notice the mistakes in my beloved film. I let it go – it was reassuring to know that Jennifer Grey had been allowed to keep her knickers on for the scene, in many ways. At least they were treating their actresses right.

The joy of obsessing over something you love is that there are always new things to discover, that take you back and give you an excuse to watch it again. The more I delve into the stories behind *Dirty Dancing* – the difficulties, the challenges – the more I admire it, and the more I love it. It's a relationship that never gets old or remains static because you can keep it alive with little morsels of gossip, or shared moments with other fans, new experiences, and a decent dose of nostalgia. *Dirty Dancing* is like an old friend to me now, but like the best kind of old friends, you never get tired of spending time together. The spark is still there, even after all these years.

9
Kellerman's Anthem

Day 1

The flight into Roanoke, Virginia, is bumpy. The plane is small, and there is a huge storm gathering over the Blue Ridge Mountains. As we bounce around, the wings swinging from side to side, I think to myself, 'It's OK, if it was dangerous, they would have cancelled the flight.' After another downward thump, and a sudden drop through the sky, followed by unnerving whirring and scraping sounds, I wonder whether *Dirty Dancing* is worth dying for and decide, on balance, it is.

When we land, I discover the previous six flights were, in fact, cancelled, and this is the first one that has been allowed to land all day. In some ways I am pleased, because this is the only way I could have got to Kellerman's in time for the start of the *Dirty Dancing* themed weekend I am headed for. But mostly, I am simply relieved to be on the ground.

Rewind to six months ago: I am noodling around on the internet, looking for information about *Dirty Dancing*, as I have just had all my dreams come true and been given a publishing deal to write this very book. 'I wonder where the real Kellerman's is,' I thought, as I started work on the first chapter, feeling slightly embarrassed that I had never looked before. I guess I had always assumed it only really existed in the film. It takes about three seconds to tap it into the search box, and then there it is, right in front of me. The place is called Mountain Lake Lodge. It is in an area called Pembroke, Virginia, near the town of Blacksburg. And though it usually operates as a normal hotel, offering all sorts of outward bound activities in the surrounding forest, they also host four themed weekends a year, where everything is about *Dirty Dancing*. There is one in April, and I know there and then that I absolutely have to go.

And now I am in a car with Bob, the very courteous driver, who will take me from Roanoke's tiny airport to the very place. I want to say we are 'speeding through the Virginia countryside', but really we are driving at a responsible and sedate pace, such is Bob's considerate style of chauffeuring. He tells me that the local rumour is Jennifer Grey has recently moved to a neighbouring area, considered one of the most rural parts of the United States, and famed for its hippy communes. I wonder whether she ever drops into Kellerman's for a beer for old time's sake. I later discover this is highly unlikely to happen . . .

After an hour or so, we are driving up a steep and winding incline, deep in the mountains. My ears actually pop as we gain altitude, and the storm has really set in by now – rain is lashing at the windows of the car. But the scene outside is still beautiful and dramatic, and we are getting ever closer. I have a mix of feelings – excitement, anticipation, some residual fear of losing my life after that landing. I don't feel worried that I will be let down by the experience ahead though; I am not concerned that I will not enjoy it, or that it will not be all that I dreamed. For some reason, I can already sense that the magic of Kellerman's is strong. I find I am smiling. This is going to be great. And then, here we are.

We pull around the back, so although it feels vaguely familiar, the full effect of being in this iconic place will have to wait. Bob takes my bag, wishes me well, and he's gone. I walk into the reception area and gasp. It's Kellerman's. Actual Kellerman's. I can see through the open doorway into the restaurant, the very restaurant where the Housemans sat to eat their meals. It is teasing me, but I have admin to do first. I can't just take a run at it right now. I try to look dignified and cool. This pose will not last long.

The woman checking in ahead of me is wearing a *Dirty Dancing* t-shirt and is showing the receptionist her watermelon manicure – each fingernail has been painted to resemble a slice of the fruit. All the staff are wearing Kellerman's t-shirts and, as I look around, I notice that everyone in the lobby has some kind of themed *Dirty Dancing* clothing on. I pat my bag, glad of my Baby costume, and the Kellerman's t-shirt I bought from the live show merchandise stall back in March.

I thought I'd be too embarrassed to wear it, but now I see I would be more embarrassed not to.

I can't wait to look around. The check-in is smooth and soon I am in my room. I don't have a cabin, but that's OK because there is only one of me, and I can see already that the place is busy. I dump my bags and look out of my window. Is that . . .? It can't be . . . but it looks like . . . it looks like BABY'S CABIN, with its distinctive green roof and white balustrade. Oh god, I think it is, I think it is. I am here, I can see it from my window. I picture her in there, with Jake, and Marge and Lisa. The rain is still pouring. I remember the scene where Lisa says, 'I'm so sick of this rain,' and Baby pulls her coat on to leave. I can hardly believe what I am looking at.

I pull on my coat to leave – rain or no rain, I want to get outside to see it all for real. Walking back through the lobby, I can see that there is now a queue of people waiting to check in. There are people greeting each other like old friends and it is clear that they have been to these weekends before. The atmosphere is warm – after all, as we know, 'old friends are the best'. The staff (THE STAFF!) are setting up the restaurant for the dinner later, so I can't go in, but I get another tantalising peek. Later on, I will be sat at one of those tables. I wonder if they are putting a pickle on everybody's plate.

I walk through the bar and find a door to the outside. I cross the driveway, and see at once that this is where the Housemans pulled up to be met by Max Kellerman. 'So, I finally got you up on my mountain!' he says. This is where Baby helps Billy unload a suitcase from the boot of the car – 'Hey, you want a job here?'

Lines like this from the film are sliding through my mind all the time – I can't help it. I take some steps down to a small lawn and turn back to face the hotel. And OH MY GOD. THERE IT IS. It's Kellerman's. Utterly unchanged – that distinctive thick grey stone, that chimney rising, the awnings, the shutters. I just stand and stare for a moment, though the wind and rain are lashing at my face. I feel that I have entered a wonderful dream. It's as if I have stepped into the film by some magic, like a character in a Roald Dahl book. I have become part of it. I think I may finally have found my 'happy place'.

I take a photo and put it on Twitter, 'Uh, guys . . . I'm at Kellerman's' I write to caption the picture, and my timeline goes nuts. Within a couple of minutes it has nearly a thousand likes, and is climbing all the time. There are various gasped replies – 'OMFG! I didn't know it was an actual place!' many people say, and I resolve there and then to share as much as I can. Because it is an actual place, and I am in it.

I realise I am now soaked to the skin; my M&S raincoat is not as waterproof as advertised. My legs are a little wobbly, and I am warm inside, but still, this is not the kind of weather you want to be standing around in. It famously rained throughout the filming in Virginia, and I can suddenly relate on a very direct level. Perhaps a little too direct. I decide to go inside – to go INSIDE KELLERMAN'S – and find a drink. I need a drink.

The bar is filling up but there is one stool left, so I sit on it and open the drinks menu. There is a list of *Dirty Dancing* themed cocktails and I order a 'Kellerman's' from the friendly barman. Sitting alongside me are two couples who are chatting about a walk they went on that day around the lake. I wonder if this is The Lake, as in the actual lake, but I don't want to butt in.

My drink is served and I take a sip. I can confirm that the Kellerman's cocktail is strong, but the hit of alcohol is welcome. It also has the required loosening effect, and soon I am chatting with the two couples, who are all firefighters from Jacksonville, Florida, here on a birthday treat for one of the women, Brielle. Her husband Jay asks me who I am and where I'm from, and so now they all know I am a comedian from the UK who is a writing a book about *Dirty Dancing*. They call Terence the barman back over and tell him to show me his treasures.

A moment later, I am holding a copy of the hotel ledger from 1986 that shows Patrick Swayze stayed in room 232, and a copy of the actual shooting script, dog-eared but intact. I turn through it as if it is a sacred document and find the page where Baby says, 'I carried a watermelon.' Except the line is, 'I carried the watermelon.' Did she say it wrong on the day? Or was it an authorised change? I ask Terence but he doesn't know, perhaps we will never know. Such is the way legends are created – with a sense of mystery.

The cocktail is kicking in now and I feel an urge to lie down. I have been up since 4am due to jet lag and the adrenaline is subsiding, which makes me feel exhausted. Brielle invites me to join their table for dinner, and I accept gladly before stumbling off to my room for a quick nap.

Dinner is served. The room is buzzing with enthusiastic

Dirty Dancing chat. Everyone is wearing a t-shirt with a quote from the film printed on it, including the ladies at my dinner table. They have had them specially made. The men are wearing them too – big beefy guys who put out fires for a living are happily discussing their favourite scene in sparkly pink t-shirts with *Dirty Dancing* picked out in glitter and sequins. I feel incredibly happy. At first I was a little self-conscious talking about the film, but I now realise everyone here is as obsessed as I am. I relax into it, like a warm bath.

At one point, I look around in wonder and say out loud, 'Guys, we are eating dinner in the Kellerman's restaurant,' and they all spontaneously whoop and cheer. We have only met a couple of hours before, and we are probably worlds apart in all other respects, but here we meet with a shared love, and I feel we are friends if not for life, then at least for the weekend.

After dinner there is a costume dance party in the barn. We get changed and head over. There are about 15 women of varying size all dressed as Baby in the final scene, dancing together in the middle of the room, and the word 'hen party' springs to mind. But it is all so joyous you just want to join in. I start grooving around with my new friends and, though I held high hopes for my chances in the costume competition (I have the Baby outfit from the very cover of this book with me, along with my secret weapon – the watermelon cushion I bought from the live show merchandise stand that I thought I'd never find a use for), I already know I've lost when a woman walks in, dressed as Johnny Castle. She's quite sexy. The appeal of Johnny is so strong that even a middle-aged woman can exert some pull when she gets that quiff, sunglasses and leather jacket look going. It's the magic of this place – it covers everything in stardust.

She wins, of course. I decide it is time for me to go and trip back to my room, eyes as big as saucers. The mountain air is cool and the crickets are chirruping in the dark. I keep my eyes peeled for signs to the staff quarters, forbidding entry for guests, but I see none. I am carrying my own watermelon of course, just in case, but it seems it will not get me anywhere tonight. I reach my room, and take a last longing look at Baby's cabin out of my window. The lights are on, and it glows in the distance. 'They could really be in there now,' I think sleepily, still slightly drunk from the cocktails, and fall into bed.

Day 2

I wake up bright and early, and am the first one down to breakfast. I have had three separate and quite intense dreams about *Strictly Come Dancing* pro Kevin Clifton, so need a couple of coffees to shake it off. My subconscious is clearly processing the jumble of emotions and information coming at me.

I bump into Terence the barman, here at the crack of dawn presumably to start assembling ingredients for the extremely strong cocktails he serves, and he gives me some exciting news: the executive chef at Kellerman's, Mike Porterfield, actually worked here in 1986, during the filming of *Dirty Dancing*, and if I come back a little later, he might be willing to talk me to about those heady days. I am now one degree of separation from Baby Houseman and Johnny Castle. I can practically touch them, or at least the hand that touched them. I agree immediately.

It is a beautiful day, as if the storm had never happened. I pull on my Kellerman's t-shirt and head out into the grounds. There is an itinerary for anyone who wants some organised activity, and so I briefly join the lawn games going on in the exact spot where the 'lawn games' in the film were shot. We do the bunnyhop and throw some quoits, but sadly, there is no 'charades in the West Lobby', and I decide to move on. There's just too much to see to be penned into one place for long.

Dotted around the grounds are small placards on posts that tell you the exact scene that was filmed in that spot. There are ten of them, and I resolve to find them all. Going on at the same time is a tour by Peggy, a *Dirty Dancing* weekend legend, who knows all the gossip and is a fount of knowledge. She comes here every time the hotel puts on a *Dirty Dancing* weekend and conducts these tours out of the goodness of her heart. A group has gathered around her and is hanging on her every word as she runs through some of the behind-the-scenes info we all love ('If you notice in the last scene, Patrick's hair goes from dry when he is dancing on stage with Baby to wet when he jumps off – this is because they had to film the dance so many times he was sweaty, but they didn't have time to dry off . . .'). We ooh and ahhh and nod at each other discreetly.

I find – due to my own research and level of geekery – that I already know quite a lot of what Peggy is saying, so I break away for a little while. I head down the path leading away from the Main House ('Mom, Dad, I'm going up to the

Main House to look around' ringing in my ears every time I think the words 'Main House') and suddenly I find I am standing right in front of the gazebo where Baby confronts her father. It is unmistakable. I gulp with unexpected emotion. I have always found it a very strong and moving scene, so beautifully played by both of them – powerful and dignified – and now I am standing at the threshold of this otherwise empty wooden structure.

I walk into it. I stand in the exact place Jake Houseman sits as he listens to Baby with tears in his eyes: 'But you let me down too, Daddy. You let me down too . . .' In my mind, when I watched the film, this was always much further away from everything else, but in fact it is very close to both Baby's cabin, and the Main House.

I walk slowly around it, and then stand where Baby stands to deliver her devastating monologue. This is also where the first group dance lesson took place with Penny, ('God wouldn't have given you maracas if he didn't want you to SHAKE 'EM!'), and also the scene where Baby comes to get Johnny, who is dancing with Vivian, when she discovers Penny crying in the kitchen. I can see the interior beams are studded with fairy lights (currently off) and wonder (somewhat ridiculously) whether these were the very bulbs that made that night-time dance so magical. I haven't felt this excited in years.

The geography of the place is foreshortened. I realise that from where I stand, I am looking at the lake, the very lake where they practised the lift. Again, the implication in the film is that they had to drive some distance from Kellerman's to reach the water, but it is right here, and you can see it from the gazebo. I should be experienced enough in filming by now to understand the way you can position a camera to trick the eye, and sure enough, if I move my eye-line, you can't see the lake from the gazebo anymore, but it is still somehow a surprise, because the film is so real to me.

I reluctantly leave the gazebo – I don't know why but the energy is strong in there – and head over to the edge of the lake. Peggy and her group are within earshot again, and I hear her telling everyone that the level of the water is much lower than it was during the filming. This is apparently normal for a mountain lake, and the water comes and goes with its own rhythm. I gaze out at it, wondering whether the homeopaths are right, and if water does hold memory. If so, then this particular body of H2O has seen a lot.

The day is warm, but there is still a fresh chill in the air, and I can quite see how the lake could have been so cold that it turned the actors' lips blue, and Grey became ill following the scene. One of the staff members later confirms to me that no matter the weather, the water is always freezing. But this is the exact spot where it all happened. And when I say 'the exact spot', I really mean it. One of the benefits of the reduced water level is that it has revealed the cinder blocks Patrick Swayze stood on to lift Jennifer Grey out of the water. I look over, and sure enough, on a swampy bit of grass and grit are four or five cement bricks, just sitting there like debris. I know I must go over there and stand on them myself, even if it means ruining my shoes.

When I get there, some other guests have had the same idea. I wait while they take pictures of each other, and then they offer to take a picture of me standing on them too. I hand over my phone, and carefully place my feet where Patrick placed his, over 30 years ago. I raise my arms above my head, and they snap away. They hand my phone back to me, and I take a close-up of my feet. I stay here for a moment, drinking it all in. It is so delicious. I try to feel the energy in the stones – do they resonate with some memory? Do I? I am certainly vibrating at a higher frequency than usual as I step off, back into the mud, and head over to Baby's cabin.

It is still a working hotel, I remind myself, and this cabin is available for guests to rent. I approach that distinctive white porch, where Johnny goes to make peace with Jake and is rebutted, but I see a sign saying I should not go any further. So I ignore it, and creep onto the porch itself, staying long enough for a quick selfie before I hear a sound inside and scurry away. I tell myself it is the Housemans, preparing for lunch. It's possible I am losing my mind, but in the best possible way. There is something slightly hallucinatory about this whole place.

Moving on, I find the small white posts and chain link fence that Baby, Johnny, and Billy step over to go find Penny. The placard tells me that these were put in by the filming crew, and the hotel decided to keep them. Well, they do look nice. When I turn around through 180 degrees, I see I am also now in the exact spot where the Houseman's car pulls up at the beginning of the film, to be greeted by Max Kellerman ('If it wasn't for your father, I'd be standing here dead!').

By now I am Tweeting all my selfies, and the response is huge and joyful (hello if you Tweeted me that day!). I feel afresh how privileged I am to be here, on this most personal of pilgrimages.

As I walk on, I hear Peggy telling her group that the awnings and the shutters on the hotel were also added by the production, and I imagine Mountain Lake Lodge was glad of the refit, even if the filming was inconvenient. The place is clearly doing well, as a larger pool and some new cabins are being built, maybe to accommodate people like me. Since the film was re-released in 1997 (bizarrely, as a result of a campaign headed by US chat show host Conan O'Brien – who knew he was such a fan?!), it has experienced a new wave of popularity, and these weekends get busier and busier.

I head back inside and have a moment in the restaurant. One of the waiting staff tells me that the light fittings and the tables are the same as in 1986. I find the spot where Baby pours water over Robbie, and the table the Housemans sit at when Jake tells his family they will be leaving early. I pose in the doorway where Baby sees Max Kellerman brief his waiting staff, when Johnny walks in to annoy Robbie and receives a dressing-down from the boss. There is a placard for the table the Housemans sit at for dinner on their first night, and you can see from the production still photo nailed to the wall above it that almost nothing has changed.

I am now on my way through the hotel to find room 232, the one Patrick Swayze stayed in during the filming. It is upstairs, and I creep along the empty corridor, aware that someone is probably staying in that room, and I may not be allowed to stand outside it for too long, or take a picture here. I need to be quick and sneaky, I think.

I find the room, and take a quick look around. No one is here, so I stand in front of the door and raise my phone in selfie mode. At this precise moment, out of nowhere, the receptionist appears – a lovely middle-aged lady in a Kellerman's t-shirt – and I drop my phone. I can't think of a way to style this out, so I just apologise, in anticipation of a telling-off. Instead, she smiles at me and says in her soft Virginia drawl, 'Would y'all like a picture outside of Patrick's room, honey?' And I nod, grateful but slightly embarrassed. She takes three and hands the phone back. 'You have a wonderful time now,' she says, and heads off back to work. I stay here for a moment. RIP, beautiful Patrick.

I skip lunch to have a wander around the wilder part of the grounds. And suddenly, here is the very place where Baby finds the sign forbidding her entry to the staff quarters, which she ignores, only to encounter Billy with his three watermelons. This is the moment, the transgressive moment, where instead of obeying like a good girl and turning away, curiosity gets the better of her and suddenly we have a movie.

I run my hand over the wooden fence where the sign was placed (it has now gone, but you can see a faint outline). In film writing, we sometimes call it the 'inciting incident', where the 'protagonist' (i.e. the hero) makes a decision that kicks everything off, and will change their lives. This is it – this moment, where Baby moves past the sign forbidding her from entering, is the inciting incident. This is where it all begins. I take a selfie. Obviously.

The next part of the scene was filmed at another location, as was much of the film. The two main locations were this one, and a place in North Carolina called Lake Lure. So sadly there is no way for me to find the steps she and Billy walk up to the party, or the wooden steps she later dances up (now on private property), or the white bridge she throws herself across (it has been dismantled). The gymnasium where the final scene with the lift was shot was also in North Carolina, and has since burned down. A small piece of the wooden floor was saved and is now in the lobby of a hotel there. This was also where the famous 'corner' Baby was put in was, and so there is no chance of sitting in it here. Johnny's cabin, and most of the staff quarters, are also in Lake Lure, North Carolina, and are available to visit. For me, this will have to be another time.

But there is plenty to keep me excited here in Virginia. And looking up the path, away from the 'Watermelon' location, it feels strangely familiar. It inclines up and away, and as I walk up it, I know I am right – this is the path where Baby pulls Johnny down as her father emerges unexpectedly from the hotel below, with Robbie and Lisa. It's where Johnny realises she is ashamed of him, and they have an argument. I feel particularly smug about finding this, as there is no placard here. I have done this all by myself, with only my obsessive knowledge of the film as my guide. I take a lot of pictures of what to most people may look like a dirt track above a white door, but to me is an important moment in the evolution of Baby and Johnny's relationship.

It is now time for the afternoon dance lesson, so I head over to the barn. It is full of people already, and my firefighter friends from Florida are there, all in a fresh batch of *Dirty*

Dancing t-shirts. A lady instructor has commenced the lesson, and we learn a basic salsa routine. I am not very good at it, but that is mainly because I am not concentrating properly. I can't quite get my head around all that I have seen. I also don't have a partner, so it's difficult to follow the moves.

Then suddenly, Dennis, also an instructor, is upon me, taking me into hold and patiently explaining how the turn works. He is very kind and tolerant of my ineptitude, but once or twice I manage to get it right, and he is pleased. I can't in truth say the lady instructor is a Penny, or that Dennis is a Johnny, but then I am no Baby, so we take what we find. It is unlikely that there will be any steamy affairs, is what I'm saying, but on balance that is probably a good thing, as although my husband is very tolerant of my love for *Dirty Dancing*, I don't want to push the experience too far. It's a good dance lesson in any case, and my friends are also having a great time. The men are trying incredibly hard to get it right for their wives, and I find it quite moving and sweet.

Once the lesson is over, I can go back to the hotel to meet Terence the barman, who I have arranged to have a little chat with on his break. I pass the archway where Johnny drives his black car away in the rain (the wrong direction, apparently, as the hotel operates a strict one-way policy) and take a quick picture.

Terence shows me to a quiet spot, and tells me he has someone he would like me to meet. Out comes Mike Porterfield, now the executive chef at Mountain Lake Lodge, and we sit down together. Mike was working here in 1986, and in a further twist, grew up here too, as his family owned the hotel in the first part of the twentieth century. He got to know Patrick Swayze, and often hung out with him. In fact, he said Patrick was incredibly friendly and kind to everyone, calling anyone he met 'Buddy' and asking to bum a cigarette or share a beer on the veranda after a hard day. Mike even gave Patrick a lift into town on his motorbike (he still has the very one), scaring him somewhat on the winding mountain road with the sheer drop to one side. He says with a glint in his eye, 'I race motorbikes, so I thought I'd give him an experience . . .' I can imagine what this 'experience' was like, as it was scary enough driving that road with good old Bob in charge of a Ford Sedan, going at 30mph.

But as friendly as Patrick was, it seems Jennifer was at the other end of the spectrum, and indeed I overhear from someone that a request from the hotel for her to come down one *Dirty Dancing* weekend, and maybe sign some autographs, was met with a brisk lawyer's letter telling them never to make contact again. I can't verify this, but it does seem to represent the difference between the two actors, and how they approached the filming and the success of *Dirty Dancing*.

Mike also tells me that they filmed the scene with Penny crying in the kitchen here, the very kitchen he is now in charge of. I take care to compliment him on his ravioli from the night before (not a euphemism), and then ask the thing he knows I'm going to ask – he doesn't miss much, does Mike. 'Can I . . . I mean, could I . . . I mean, I know you're very busy but . . .' He lets me run on, a mischievous smile forming on his lips – he's going to make me say it. 'Would it be possible to see that spot . . . you know, for the book I'm writing?' Yeah right, 'for the book I'm writing'. It's for me. It's all for me, we both know this.

He hesitates for a moment (pure drama), makes me wait a second, and then says, 'Depends how early you can get down here in the morning . . .'

'I can get here as early as you like,' I say breathlessly, and I mean it.

'Seven, then,' he says. 'Seven sharp, before it gets busy for breakfast.'

I am elated – for the first time I bless my jet lag. Seven?! Seven is a lie-in. I've been getting up at 4 am most days. 'I'll be there,' I say, 'thank you, thank you so much.' He nods and is gone. He's seen it all before.

The day is drawing to a close. I have met a lady called Elaine from Glasgow at the dance class who is also here alone. She tells me she is recently divorced, and has taken herself on holiday here as it is not something her former husband would have done with her. My new Florida-friends agree instantly to have her at their dinner table, along with me. 'You're family now, Miss Katy,' they say, and once again I am grateful for that American sense of generosity and hospitality.

We meet at the table at 7pm, and they say grace and hand round small cups of homemade moonshine to get us in the mood. I do short interviews with each of them, as I want to know what they love about the film. They are all enthusiastic, and Randy, the biggest and I would say the oldest of the group, brings me up short with his answer to 'What is your favourite scene and why?'. In his strong Florida accent, looking every inch the tough guy, he says, 'I love the scene where Baby confronts her father. I love that she stands up to him. I have three daughters, and if they ever stand up to me like that, I will be so proud.'

Jay, another firefighter says, 'I love the scene where Baby first dances with Johnny because we see her become a woman for the first time.' The ladies give good answers too, but something about these guys abandoning themselves to the message of the film is weirdly touching.

Almost all the waiting staff are students from Virginia Tech, the local university campus. One of our group starts teasing our waitresses, Toni and Tyler, about where the staff after-party is that night. They deflect it a couple of times, but in the end, they say doubtfully, 'Well, I mean, we have parties down at Virginia Tech sometimes, but it's a bit of a drive . . .' They look totally baffled, and it suddenly dawns on me – they haven't seen the film. They have no idea what we're talking about. The term 'staff after-party' means absolutely nothing to them. I ask how old they are – 20 and 22 respectively. I ask why they have never seen *Dirty Dancing*, not even once. They look a little embarrassed, and I don't mean it as a confrontation, I am just curious. They both say the same thing: it just doesn't feel relevant. To them, it's an 'old film', and they like different stuff – sci-fi and so on. *Harry Potter* is the big coming-of-age movie for them. I explain that *Dirty Dancing* is one of the few coming-of-age movies for girls, and they nod politely, but I don't think it's going in. I feel a little deflated. I look around – everyone here is way over 40. I hope it doesn't die with my generation.

We finish up and head over to the barn for a final dance

party. The dance instructors put on a show, based on the film, which everyone loves, and then the floor opens up to all of us. One of my Florida firefighter friends gallantly asks me to dance, which we do for the final moments of a song, but as 'Hungry Eyes' starts up, I take my leave. I'm not sure even the most accommodating of wives is going to want to watch her husband dance to that song with another woman.

Sure enough, as I move away, they come together. I watch them for a moment. It's a lovely scene. I stay to sing the rest of 'Hungry Eyes' with Elaine (we both know all the words, obviously), and then I head back to my room. I stop off on the way to admire Kellerman's at night, lit up from the inside. I feel lit up from the inside, too.

Day 3

I had my alarm set for 6.30am just in case, but true to form, I am awake from 4.30. At five to seven I go down to the kitchen for my appointment with Mike the chef. The place is deserted. I knock on the door and enter the kitchen. THE KITCHEN! I look around, trying to get my bearings, but I am lost. Then Mike appears – I can tell he is slightly surprised I have made it in time, but he gives me a huge smile and leads me to the very place. He even clears a few bits and pieces away to make it look how it did in the film. I am rooted to the spot. It really is exactly the same. This is where Penny is sat crying, when Baby is led in here by Neil Kellerman to find some after-hours food.

I turn to Mike and, although I feel a bit embarrassed

– this is, after all, his place of work, and I am conscious of breakfast service approaching – I know I have to ask. 'Do you mind taking a picture of me if I sit there?' He nods, and I take my place, even pretending to cry a bit, like Penny. He takes the photos, and then shows me the fridges Baby and Neil stand at, and the corridor of stainless-steel counters Johnny sweeps down to rescue Penny. There is no placard here – it something very few people get to see.

I thank him and leave him to get on with the day. Soon, my trip will be over. I float over to the breakfast hall, and take a large coffee and a couple of boiled eggs. As I wait in line for a bagel to toast, a woman spontaneously says out loud, 'Sylvia?' And I automatically say back, 'Yes, Mickey' and we both laugh. That's what it's like here – a little community. The love just pours out of everyone. We are on a spiritual retreat of sorts, and it is now coming to an end.

In the dining room, a huge screen is set up where they are playing *Dirty Dancing*. I sit quietly, munching my eggs and taking it all in. A lady comes over to me and says, 'Excuse me, has anyone ever told you, you look like a famous actress?' I say I don't know – which actress is that? She says, 'From a movie called *Walking on Sunshine*.' I laugh and say, 'Yes, because that's me!' She is delighted, and I think to myself that this must be one of the only places in the world where anyone is going to recognise me from the musical I made in Italy, which largely sank without trace. This is the same demographic. It's my demographic. Because it's me, too.

As I watch *Dirty Dancing* playing out, I feel so content and happy, I don't want to leave, and I just sit with everyone else, enjoying the watermelon scene. As luck would have it, Toni the millennial waitress who has never seen the film is working at breakfast this morning. She takes my plate and asks me whether I have got some good stuff for my book (they all know by now what I am doing here). I say, 'Oh yes, thanks – so much, so, so much.' She must think we're all crazy.

She stands next to me for a minute, and we watch together. 'You know, you're kind of watching *Dirty Dancing* right now,' I say quietly. She nods. 'Maybe have a look at it sometime. It's a rite-of-passage film about a teenage girl becoming a woman. There aren't many of those around – where the girl is the hero. It's quite important in some ways. It has a strong message.' She nods again. I tell myself she looks kind of curious, but perhaps that is wishful thinking on my part.

I pack up my stuff and check out. Dani, on reception, asks me whether I have seen the hotel ledger from 1986, with Patrick's name on it, and his room number. I have a copy of it, I tell her. She also asks whether I know that they have a version of the original shooting script at the hotel. I nod again, and say I saw it on Friday night. 'Oh, so you know the ending is different in the script.' Record scratch. Wait, what? 'Yes, it's different. In the script, it doesn't end with the lift . . .'

I check my watch. Ten minutes until my taxi arrives to take me back to Roanoke airport. That's just enough time to go back to the bar and find Terence and, if he will let me, take another look at that script. When I first saw it on Friday, I didn't think to look at the end – I just looked at the watermelon scene.

I race across the lobby. Terence is there, cleaning and chatting with guests. I pull him to one side and ask him for the script again. He nods silently, responding to my urgent tone, and slides it across to me in its cellophane wrapping. Aware of the clock ticking, I leaf through the delicate pages to the final scene. Here it is – 'Nobody puts Baby in a corner', yes, yes, then Marge Houseman, 'I think she gets this from me', yes, yes, then the dance, and the lift, yes, then Jake saying, 'You looked wonderful out there.' Everyone floods the dance floor, and then . . . and then ANOTHER FOUR PAGES.

Johnny and Baby are talking. My eyes swim a little, what are they saying? What's this? They are discussing their future? They are saying the world will be against them? But somehow they will make it work? And then Baby and Lisa are in the car, and Lisa is saying, 'What's sex like, Baby?' and Baby is saying, 'It's better than dirty dancing,' and then Marge Houseman, from the front seat, says wistfully, 'I always wished I had a sister.' THE END.

And with a whoosh, I know I have been right all along – this is a film about dancing, yes, but also sex, how great sex can transform your life, and how women look after each other – especially sisters. This weekend, Mountain Lake Lodge has been mostly populated by women – they are 90 per cent of the clientele. There have been some wonderful men here – men who get it, who really get it – but it's about the women.

As I drive away from Kellerman's, and this wonderful, exhilarating dream, I find myself hoping that 20-year-old Toni the waitress will watch *Dirty Dancing* sometime, and tell all her young friends to do the same. They are right in it, here at Kellerman's, every night. They don't know what they're missing.

I went to the *Dirty Dancing* weekend for reasons of research, and also because I thought it would be fun. I didn't expect to feel so emotional though, so *happy*. Sometimes when you visit places where a favourite film has been shot, it can make the movie feel less real somehow – it destroys the magic. But in fact, the opposite was true here. In many ways, *Dirty Dancing* now feels more real to me. I felt that I was within it for a couple of days, that perhaps I was Baby – or at least, Baby was nearby. I think all the people I met had the same feeling: the spirit of Johnny, and Penny, and the Housemans, and our heroine herself lingers everywhere. You feel that if you could just turn quickly enough, you might catch one of them disappearing behind a bush, or hurrying up a track, or diving into the lake. It feels almost . . . haunted, but in a good way. *Dirty Dancing* inhabits every corner of this place. It's wonderful.

And yes, before you ask, I absolutely had the time of my life.

10
(I've Had) The Time of My Life

To return for a moment to where we started, when my husband said to me, on that night of my fortieth birthday, 'What would you like to do this evening?' and I spontaneously said, having already feasted on Chinese takeaway and champagne (couldn't get a babysitter . . .), 'I'd like to watch *Dirty Dancing*, please,' I didn't realise how emotional it would make me. Looking back now, I think I somehow felt it would complete the circle, or at least send me into the second half of my life (fingers crossed I make it to 80, anyway) with as much force as it did the first. It felt like the right moment for a reckoning – with my teenage self and also with the film. Was it really as good as I thought it was? Had I outgrown it? I was genuinely worried. I didn't want it to let me down. Or, in fact, to have let it down myself.

I didn't fear turning 40 – in fact, I was quite looking forward to it because in some respects I've felt 40 years old since I was 15. A friend of mine once told me a theory that everyone has 'an age they're meant to be'. For example, some people are just brilliant at being 16. They peak at school, they're popular, whatever the fashion of the moment is fits them perfectly, they seem to have an innate understanding of how social politics and love and sex, and all that stuff works at a teenage level. They have a great time until they're 20, and then it often stalls and they effectively live the same life as they did at 16 for the rest of their lives – marry a school sweetheart, buy a house in the town they grew up in, go to the same pubs and clubs. I watched these people with a certain amount of awe and envy at the time. They seemed to have some sort of secret, which I assumed would last forever, but it doesn't.

I, on the other hand, stomped my way through my teenage years, frumpy and furious, with a lot to prove, a desire to show off, and a serious superiority complex that made my company a bit of an acquired taste. In fact, I actually told a family friend that I was an 'acquired taste' at the age of 13, when he implied that I was being a bit bolshie. Just take that in for a moment – can you imagine what a room-silencing comment that was from a pubescent girl? I even remember flicking my hair and wriggling smugly in my chair when I said it. What a dick.

Then there are those who are great at being 25 – they travel the world, take a few risks, party a lot, have as much sex as they like without feeling any guilt or shame, and look amazing yet also casual in a bikini. They give good Instagram. I was not one of those either. I was full of drive and ambition, to a charmless degree, and while I went out a lot and had fun, I was also constantly worried that I would not achieve what I had set out to, which made me pushy, intense and a bit paranoid. I did not take care of my health on any level. I was full of fear too, that whatever success I did manage was based on a false premise and that I simply wasn't good enough for the job. I looked neither amazing nor casual in a bikini.

But now I'm 40, I am chilling out a little bit. I got some things done, which is good and helps, but there is a greater sense of confidence, which is surely the compensation for ageing for all of us. I had a relationship with an American comedian when I was in my twenties, who sometimes regarded my somewhat pointless and futile angst about everything as being superficial. He'd rub his chin and say, 'You know, you're gonna be a bad-ass bitch when you're 40.' I tried to take it as a compliment, but it was also meant as a criticism of what I was then, and 40 felt a long way off.

Well, it's here now, and I admit I took a moment to consider my ex-boyfriend's prediction – have I managed to become a 'bad-ass bitch' at 40? A bit. Recently, for example, a man blocked my path in the street and told me to smile, and for the first time in my life I said, 'I'll smile if I want to' and walked past him. I wasn't sure if the silence behind me was a good sign (he was shocked into stillness) or a bad sign (I was about to get whacked in the back of the head) but I didn't look round, though my heart was thumping. Nice middle-class girls are not brought up to be rude to strangers.

I have also, three times in the last few years, threatened legal action to companies who didn't think they needed to pay me despite what it said in the contract, and it's always worked. I have requested more money for work when I know I'm being sold short, and I have also said I expect pay parity with men doing the same work. I have fired three people (it was a bad scene). All of this would have made me cringe ten years ago.

But I still try too hard to please, I'm more obedient than I look, and I am very bad at expressing anger to people who behave badly towards me. I'd still rather suck it up than have it out. So I walk around powered by bile batteries to some extent, which isn't good for general inflammation – no amount of turmeric latte is going to soothe the rage you feel when someone you trust fucks you over and then runs away. That fury is for the ages. I should exercise more, I still drink too much, and I'd rather spend an entire afternoon staring out of a window than anything else. There's work to do. So, roll on 50.

Who would Baby be at 40, I wonder. Who would she have been at 25? I don't think she was one of those who had her best years during her teens, although she may have already had the best sex of her life by that point, which would be sad, but at least it happened – some women never experience an orgasm at all, for god's sake. I don't think she'd have stayed with Johnny – she'd have gone 'to Mount Holyoke in the fall', and perhaps there would have been a few visits and letters, maybe even a disastrous and slightly pouty night out in a college bar with all her 'intellectual friends'. It would have fizzled, just as most teenage infatuations do. And in fact, I love this about *Dirty Dancing* – it's a happy ever after, but for her rather than 'them'. Perhaps some part of us wants them to be together, but that is only the familiar tug of a fairytale ending, ingrained in us as women from birth. And yes, there was a moment when I saw that final scene in the shooting script behind the bar at 'Kellerman's', when my heart beat faster, and I had the evidence in my hands that Bergstein originally wanted them to be together too. But a film is more than just the script, and the final version of *Dirty Dancing* is something altogether different than even the writer intended. As I said in the beginning, it's Baby's story – it's a rite-of-passage film about a teenage girl; it doesn't have to end in a wedding just because that is what we are taught about stories for girls. I'm glad it doesn't – it was the right move to cut that ending, and just take us out on the literal high of a lift.

So, it would have ended with Johnny, and she'd have travelled extensively in her twenties, seen a lot of life and gained valuable experience, maybe done some further education, and then gone into some form of public service and finally politics. I think of her at 40 as a young congresswoman with some real fire in her belly, tipped for the presidency one day. Maybe she would have become a Hillary Clinton by now, but with more social skills and less sex scandal (except for that one night with her 'old friend' Johnny Castle, years later, in a hotel in New York – they bumped into each other in the street and things . . . developed. She has never told anyone). She would have shed the name Baby, of course, and be Frances Houseman, making good on her namesake, 'the first woman in the Cabinet'. She'd read *The Fountainhead* and discard it in disgust. She'd be a bad-ass bitch.

I guess in my head, Baby is growing with me. I'm going to ignore the obvious metaphor here because it's slightly disgusting . . . actually, no – I have to say it. I have a Baby growing inside me. OK, now forget I said that – I just have to get these things out of my system sometimes. But that's the truth – Baby is now 40, because I'm 40.

Of course, I can write sequel plots, and fantasise all kinds of developments and endings for Baby and Johnny, but they exist as part of my work brain – writing stories, playing with characters. But the real Baby, who I took into my psyche as an 11-year-old girl, is right next to me all the time – when I feel young, she's young. When I feel old, she's old too.

I asked Deborah Frances-White, writer and creator of the wildly successful *The Guilty Feminist* podcast and book, and fellow life-long *Dirty Dancing* obsessive, why she thinks Baby is such an enduring icon for women. She said:

> *I argue in* The Guilty Feminist *book that the reason so many women love romcoms is not that we prefer romance to adventure, law and space – it's that it's the only genre where we can routinely find proactive female heroes. We want to see humans like us take charge and step dangerously towards action with hope and daring. The most feminist moment for me of all though is when Johnny goes to leave. Baby doesn't beg him to stay. She doesn't cry and wail and claim she can't live without him. She knows it's a summer fling.*

The beauty of this journey has been the opportunity to think about *Dirty Dancing* and how it has affected my life, and also to meet and talk to all the others who feel the same. Perhaps it is because there are so few films like this, shown entirely from a woman's perspective, where she initiates all the action, including the sex, takes full responsibility for herself and her actions, gets the guy, saves him, and then is lifted high in the air to wild applause. She is the hero of the story so completely and utterly, and so it's no wonder that the rarity of this leads to a wide and diverse fan base. We simply don't have very many of these to obsess over, so we all converge on this one. But the positive side of that is a sense of community and shared experience between hundreds of thousands of women, and men too – I have found plenty of male fans, or at least, men who love their women enough to see why it's important to us.

I watched *Dirty Dancing* alone so many times as a girl, not realising so many others were doing the same. I wore out my VHS tape (not a euphemism), and it was not until this year that I discovered how many other women did too. We watched it again and again, feeling that thrill and excitement, and that power. The thing about *Dirty Dancing* is that it has some magic ingredient that makes you feel invincible. Yes, so does cocaine, but *Dirty Dancing*'s power lasts longer and it's a lot cheaper. It is drug-like – you enter Baby's world, and you come out feeling better and stronger. What more could you want from a heroine? What more could you want from anything?

I was worried when I started looking at *Dirty Dancing* that it would not stand up to scrutiny, or that it would disappear through my fingers into nothing. But in fact, there was more packed in there than I had even imagined. It works as entertainment, yes, of course, but the political messages are as fresh and pertinent now as ever. And the lessons too are still there for any girl who wishes to heed them. I'd make it required viewing for teenage boys and girls – it should be taught in schools. The syllabus would be:

How to stand up for yourself.

How to help others without judgement.

How not to be a passenger in your own life.

What consensual sex looks like.

Women and girls can and should ask for sex without being called sluts.

Good sex means good sex for everyone.

If you want him, go get him.

Women should be sovereign over their own bodies.

Our parents are not always the heroes we think they are – they are human, like us.

Be nice to your sister as she will always help you out in the end.

One failed romance will not break you.

You should take risks and live in the moment.

A 'yes' is almost always better than a 'no' when an opportunity to learn something new is presented.
Don't let anyone put you in a corner.
You are the hero of your own story.

All of the above, I learned from *Dirty Dancing*. These lessons are present in other films, books, TV shows and plays of course, but not usually in one place. It's an addictive story, with a satisfying and yet open end. We get to write the next bit, with our own lives. I have done 40 years, I can only hope for another 40. Who knows what will happen? I'll watch *Dirty Dancing* again on my eightieth birthday and report back . . . Let's have the time of our lives, whatever we do. We are the heroes. We drive the story. We make it happen.

Acknowledgements

Thank you first and foremost to my agent, Cathryn Summerhayes, and HQ publisher Lisa Milton, who had such absolute belief and enthusiasm for this idea, and made a deal happen so fast it made my head spin. That kind of speed gives anyone doing creative work such an immense boost from the beginning that the energy can't help but be positive on starting writing. I still can't believe it. It's like a miracle.

Thanks to all who work with Cathryn at Curtis Brown for the endless help and patience with getting everything in place. Thanks to the whole team at HQ, especially Kate Fox for great early notes and reassurance, and Sophie Calder and all the publicity department for getting the word out in such a dynamic and exciting way. Thanks to all who were involved with the cover shoot and design – it was a ridiculously fun afternoon, and I am still washing bits of watermelon out of my hair.

Thanks to Liz Marvin for the sensitive and superb copy editing – you made the book 100 per cent better in every way.

Thanks to all at HarperCollins for making me feel so welcome (and throwing an excellent party!). Thanks to Mandy Ward and Kirsty Lloyd-Jones, who helped me build my career over many years. Thanks to Deborah Frances White for making some incredibly helpful points, and sending some brilliant thoughts of her own on *Dirty Dancing* which I was able to quote. Thanks to Vix Leyton for the chat about Secret Cinema. Thanks to Hadley Freeman, Tracey Thorn, and Tanya Gold for excellent quotable writing. Thanks to Irin Carmon and all the other bloggers, journalists and writers who have produced such insightful work on *Dirty Dancing* in recent years. And thanks to all those who responded on Twitter to my questions – I'm sorry I couldn't quote you all in the book.

Thanks to my husband David, the greatest first reader a writer could hope for, and to Skye and Thomas for endless joy and inspiration. Thanks to my parents and sister, Jessica, for putting up with me, and to Jessica especially for the excellent and expert advice on the cover.

Thanks to everyone who has given me all the experiences I have talked about in the book – if nothing happens, I can't write it! I hope I have been fair . . .

Thanks to all at Mountain Lake Lodge (or Kellerman's, as I will always call it) for an utterly magical *Dirty Dancing* weekend.

And finally, all thanks must go to Eleanor Bergstein, Patrick Swayze, Jennifer Grey, and everyone else who created the masterpiece that is *Dirty Dancing*.

References

1. Carmon, Irin, '*Dirty Dancing* Is The Greatest Movie Of All Time', Jezebel.com, 29 April 2010
2. Gold, Tanya, 'So where are the girls, old bean?', The *Sunday Times*, 7 September 2014
3. Eleanor Bergstein interview, 'The Back-Alley Abortion That Almost Didn't Make it into *Dirty Dancing*', *Broadly*.com, 21 August 2017
4. Eleanor Bergstein interview, 'The Back-Alley Abortion That Almost Didn't Make it into *Dirty Dancing*', *Broadly*.com, 21 August 2017
5. Eleanor Bergstein interview, 'The Back-Alley Abortion That Almost Didn't Make it into *Dirty Dancing*', *Broadly*.com, 21 August 2017
6. Eleanor Bergstein interview, 'The Back-Alley Abortion That Almost Didn't Make it into *Dirty Dancing*', *Broadly*.com, 21 August 2017
7. https://dirtydancingontour.com/cast-creative/eleanor-bergstein
8. Kolson, Ann 'Fairy Tale Without An Ending', *The New York Times*, 17 August 1997
9. Freeman, Hadley, *Life Moves Pretty Fast: The Lessons We Learned from 80s Movies*, HarperCollins, June 2016
10. Hutchinson, Kate 'Secret Cinema: *Dirty Dancing* review – the UK's biggest hen party', *Guardian*, 25 July 2016

Index

B

F

G

H

L

M

N

O

T

V

W

Z

ONE PLACE. MANY STORIES

Bold, innovative and
empowering publishing.

FOLLOW US ON:

@HQStories